Border Healing Woman

Contents

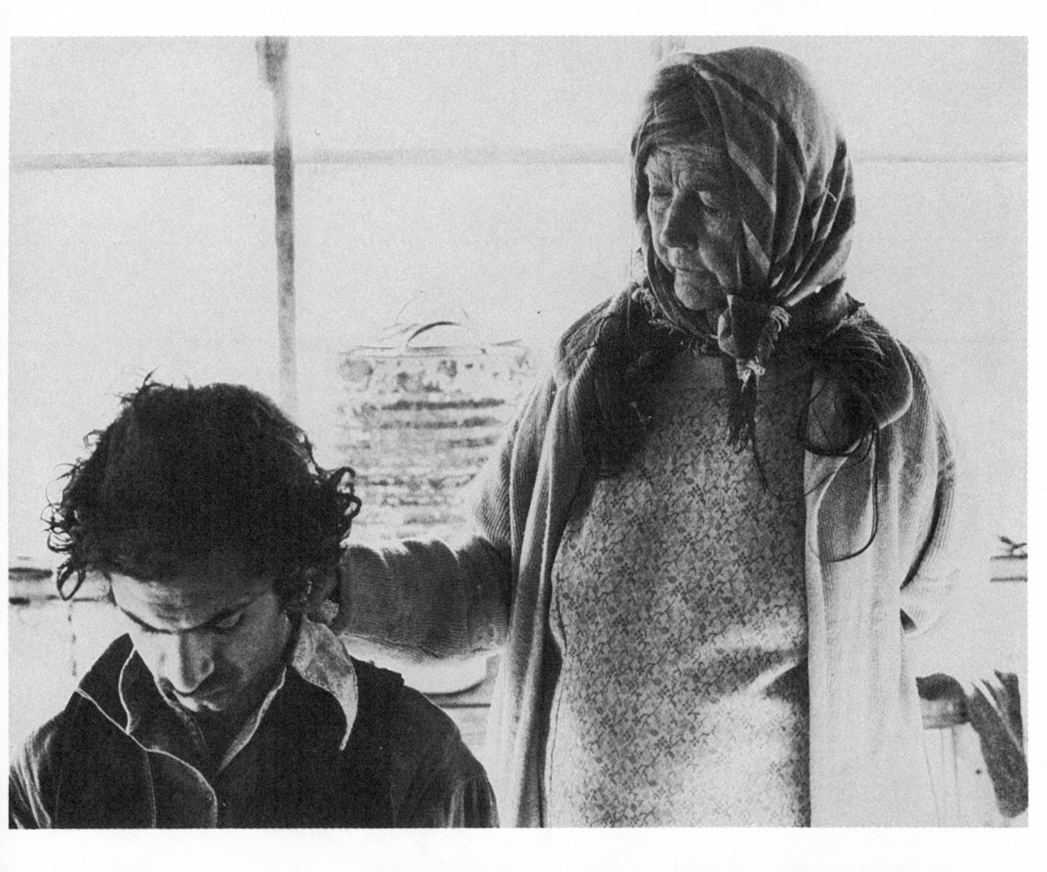

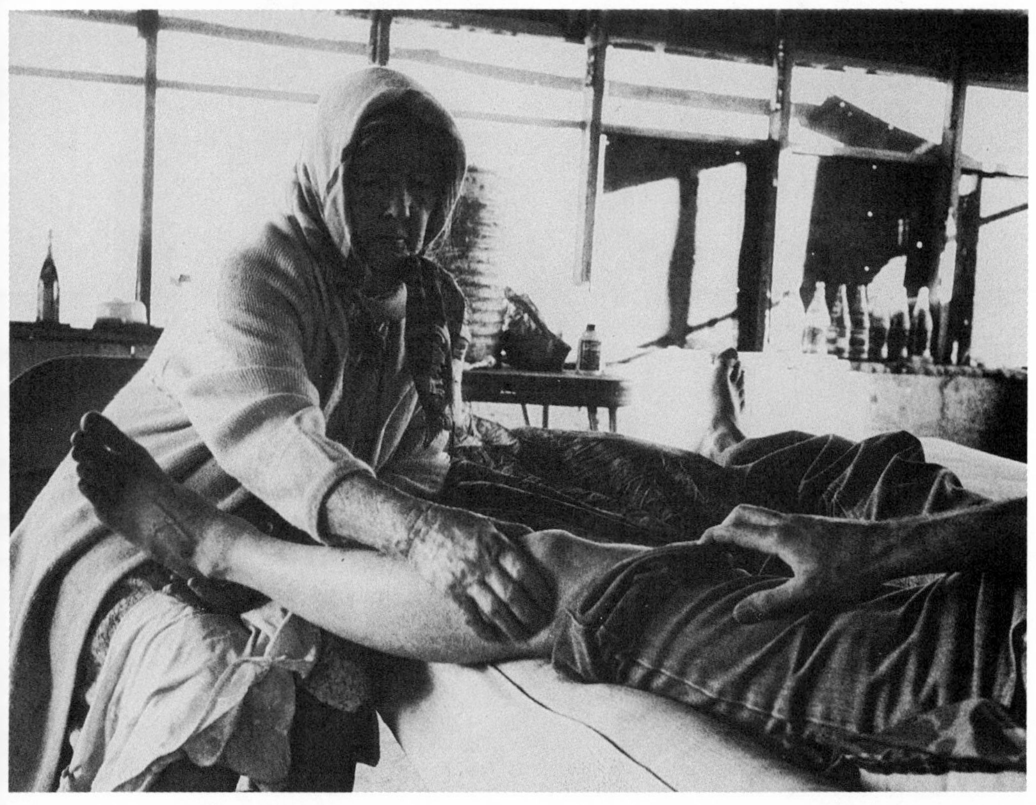

Photographs by Ann Savino

BORDER HEALING WOMAN

The Story of Jewel Babb

as told to Pat Ellis Taylor

UNIVERSITY OF TEXAS PRESS, AUSTIN

Printed in the United States of America
Fourth Paperback Printing, 1991

Requests for permission to reproduce material from this work should be sent to
Permissions
University of Texas Press
Box 7819, Austin, Texas 78713-7819

∞ The paper used in this publication meets the minimum requirements of American National Standard for Information Sciences—Permanence of Paper for Printed Library Materials, ANSI Z39.48-1984.

Library of Congress Cataloging in Publication Data
Babb, Jewel, 1900–
Border healing woman.
Bibliography: p.
1. Babb, Jewel, 1900– 2. Healers—Texas—Biography. 3. Folk medicine—Texas. 4. Healing (in religion, folk-lore, etc)—Texas. I. Taylor, Pat Ellis, 1941–
RZ408.B32A33 615.8'52'0924 [B] 80-22464
ISBN 0-292-70730-4 (pbk.)

*We no longer ask, "Has this or that been seen, heard, handled, weighed, counted, thought, and found to be logical?" We ask instead, "*Who *saw, heard or thought?"*

—CARL G. JUNG

Preface

JEWEL BABB is an eighty-year-old Anglo woman who was born in South Texas and has lived in the Texas-Mexico border area all her life. When I first heard of her, she was living in the desert approximately thirty miles from Sierra Blanca and six miles from the Rio Grande. Her name was gradually becoming known in El Paso, where I was living at the time, primarily by a large community of the Anglo counterculture who live in the upper Rio Grande valley on the Texas–New Mexico boundary line. Many of this community are interested in natural healing, herbs, and psychic phenomena. According to one story, Jewel Babb had first been discovered by Greg T., a member of the community, who had been scouting the lower Rio Grande area for peyote buttons, which, at one time, grew abundantly in the neighborhood. In the middle of the desert, he discovered her cabin and knocked on the door for water. She asked him what he was doing so far from the highway, and he answered truthfully that he was looking for peyote. "Peyote," he quotes her as saying, "will give you nothing but trouble. But I can show you some things that'll do you some good."

Since that time, the counterculture people have gone to her from El Paso in increasing numbers, not only to be cured themselves of various maladies but also to be taught her methods of using hot springs, massage, and natural healing techniques. Mrs. Babb moved from her isolated desert cabin in 1977 to a house in Valentine, Texas, which has made her more accessible to visitors. In addition to the counterculture people, Mrs. Babb is known also in the border Mexican American community and across the river in the Mexican villages. There are also many people scattered throughout the United States who came to know her during an eight-year period several years ago when she owned Indian Hot Springs, a hotel and health spa on the Rio Grande approximately eighty miles downriver from El Paso.

This book represents Mrs. Babb's life story and her views on her healing powers in her own words. The account which emerges of her developing consciousness as a faith healer is an exciting one, not only because of the insight it can provide on healers in general but also because of the model it presents of a strong, individualistic woman coming into her own powers without benefit of the support either husband or community would usually provide.

A great deal of the material in this book was transcribed orally during a three-month period when I stayed with Mrs. Babb at her Valentine home. However, Mrs. Babb also wrote long segments of the story in long hand. Her voice is weak, and she is somewhat reticent about speaking directly about herself. Thus, after long talking sessions would wear her out, she would turn to writing. We would then go over the written sections together, so that she could supplement orally in places which seemed to need elucidation. She also continued to send me additional segments whenever she would recall some incident which seemed to her to be of value in the story. I have tried to edit her writing as little as possible, other than to arrange the spoken and written segments in orderly sequence, editing no more than was absolutely necessary in order to preserve the enjoyable way of telling which is Mrs. Babb's unique "voice."

In addition to her story, I have included my own impressions of the time I spent with her and of the environment which, in my opinion, has contributed to the formation of her personality and beliefs. These personal notes have been provided so that historical and descriptive material which would provide a context for her story could be supplied and so that some idea of the circumstances under which the interviewing was done would be supplied to enable the readers to judge for themselves how these circumstances might have influenced Mrs. Babb in shaping her story. Mrs. Babb and I consider this to be a joint writing project, and we have worked equally hard in putting together a manuscript which we hope will be both informative and enjoyable. We wish to thank personally the Department of English at the University of Utah and, in particular, Dr. Hal Moore for their support in allowing me the time to pursue this project; Dr. Jan Brunvand for his encouragement; the National Endowment of the Arts for a writer's grant which allowed me time to assemble the manuscript; Dr. Elton Miles and Joe Graham of Sul Ross University for allowing me access to their files of information; Mr. and Mrs. Dogie Wright of Sierra Blanca, Texas, for the use of their personal library and for their recollections of Indian Hot Springs; Mrs. Dee Elliott for the H. L. Hunt information; W. D. Smithers for his assistance in locating material on railroad tie house construction; and Eleanor Taylor, Susie Manning, Bill Liles, and my husband, Chuck Taylor, for their continuing support of this project through long drives, desert heat, and dusty roads.

P.E.T.

Border Healing Woman

CHAPTER 1

First Visit to the Tie Camp

THE HIGHWAY between El Paso and Sierra Blanca runs through a rocky desert which rolls from horizon to horizon. Travelers on this road tend to nod to each other as their cars pass, in recognition of the only other sign of humanity for miles at a stretch. Their windows are generally rolled up, heaters on in the winter, air conditioners in the summer, radios on full volume, coolers in the back, maps in the front, trying as much as possible to ignore the view. This, at least, is the way I had traveled over this road in sporadic forays from El Paso to East Texas. In fact, although I have lived in El Paso for over fourteen years, the first trip I took into the desert itself was when Eleanor drove me to meet Jewel Babb. Eleanor had been telling me about Jewel Babb for months, describing her as an older woman who lived by herself in the desert and kept goats, who had no electricity or running water but knew the desert as well as any Indian, and who could heal people by touching them in the right places. When I told Eleanor that I wanted to meet her, she agreed to take me with her the next time she went. This first visit took place in the spring of 1975.

We drove out in Eleanor's old station wagon, which creaked and moaned on bad springs the whole trip. In the backseat were her children and mine, stacked on top of a strange assortment of goods: five gallons of water in a plastic jug, two cartons of discarded clothes we had been accumulating for the past two months, a gallon jar of honey, three loaves of whole wheat bread that Eleanor had baked, two jars of peanut butter, and an *Aloe vera* plant. This was our offering. The old clothes, according to Eleanor, Mrs. Babb cut into pieces and quilted, the food she used sparingly, and the water was a luxury her place did not have. In return she taught Eleanor about the desert and how to heal, how to use the hot springs water six miles away, and how to massage various parts of the body for health.

At Sierra Blanca, Eleanor pulled the station wagon off the highway and stopped in front of a dilapidated building at the edge of town. There was a faded barber pole by the door but no indication otherwise that it was anything but abandoned and used for storage, as the windows showed only a gray, indistinguishable clutter. Eleanor left the engine running, ducked in the low shop door, and then in a couple of minutes swung back into the driver's seat.

"She's out there," she said. "Agustín says he saw her this morning when she got her mail." Agustín T., according to Eleanor, was a barber, fiddler, sometime chauffeur and handyman, and always the combination outpost man and secretary to Jewel Babb when she was living at the tie house. Eleanor drove to the center of town, then turned south toward the Rio Grande on a blacktopped road which unexpectedly changed into packed dirt and gravel about two miles out of town. This road wandered into another and then another, so that it seemed to me that Eleanor was taking the turns almost at random. Sometimes there were large arroyos washed across the road, and we had to crawl the station wagon over them, slowing the car down to less than five miles an hour. It was hot. The children bounced up and down on the pile in the backseat, too hot even to hassle each other, their faces sweaty and red, eyes drowsy. At three, Eleanor's girl Becca was the smallest, her pudgy body perched in the middle, with Brookie, my six-year-old, on one side and Alex, Eleanor's older girl, on the other. Away from the insular highway, the desert had become totally different to me. There were small hills and valleys which we were constantly pitching up and running down into, finding the road suddenly closed in on both sides by jagged red rocks and boulders tumbled against each other. Yuccas eight and ten feet high loomed on the crests of hills, nodding to each other as if they were the incarnations of desert people friendly with each other and watchful of strangers. It was May, and there had apparently been rain, because there were blankets of yellow flowers on some of the slopes and blue and red shoots of wildflowers along the road. It was hard for me to admit that this was the same desert I had managed to avoid looking at all these years. Dozens of rabbits sprang out in several directions at the approach of the car. There were mockingbirds in the low mesquite trees which grew in the gulleys, and an occasional hawk swooped low enough for us to catch a glimpse of the white epaulets on his shoulders.

Then, rounding a slow curve, Eleanor pointed out the house to me, on a ridge about half a mile up the road. I could barely pick out the cluster of brown buildings from the clutter of desert rocks they were sitting on. As we drove closer, the details became clearer: the sheds and posts, a scattering of rusted parts of abandoned cars, the junked carcass of an old school bus. We drove into the yard between a low-lying house and a long deteriorated trailer. A black-haired man was sitting in the trailer door, but when we drove up, he turned inside and disappeared. Behind the house, I could make out a series of pens and sheds which seemed to lean against each other as their only support. Chickens bustled in the yard, and several goats were wandering freely between the buildings. The ridge dropped down quickly on all sides of the building cluster, and when we got out of the car, we could see the desert rolling off and down from us in every direction. The air was thin but hot, and no wind was blowing. This was the first human construction of any kind in the thirty miles of road we had just come over, and from this high outlook, it was the only one as far as the eye could see in all directions.

The clearing probably covered an acre of land, but, other than the various sheds, the house, and trailer, there was nothing on it for shade. Low-lying prickly pear grew in patches along the outer edges and an occasional yucca or Spanish dagger, but, otherwise, there was only rock and sand, as the goats had apparently taken care of any edible bushes or grass that had ever tried to grow here.

The main house was made of vertical railroad ties with horizontal ties at the bottom, top, and casings. It had been covered with pieces of tar paper which had been stripped off in wide sections in several places and some of these partially recovered with stamped tin panels and old license plates. But the ties were clearly visible in several places. There was a hipped roof made of boards, then covered, too, with tar paper and tin.

Eleanor walked to the screen door and knocked. The door thudded, and behind it a narrow white face with intelligent golden eyes appeared. It was a goat, apparently standing guard close to the porch. Someone called out from inside the house; then I could vaguely see a figure through the screen as the door opened.

"Why, Eleanor Taylor, you come on in here." She opened the door wide and motioned us all in. While the girls and Eleanor and I carried in the boxes from the car, she sat in a rocking chair on the porch, somewhat shy of the sudden company but smiling happily at the attention. Her skin was ruddy but relatively smooth for her age, and her hair was long and gray, gathered in a loose bun at her neck. She wore a plain housedress with a dark apron tied around her waist.

Her body was strong and vigorous, and she sat solidly, in firm possession of herself, her hands folded calmly on her lap in the midst of activities. She motioned us to sit on the porch when we finished carrying in the provisions, which she directed us to pile by the side of the door. She wouldn't allow us to go into the main part of the house. That part, she said, was too cluttered and dirty. Besides, the porch was where she lived and slept in the warm months; the house was only for when the weather was cold. The porch was screened and ran the full length of the house. On it were two iron beds piled high and soft with quilts and pillows, and to one side was her rocking chair and a square table. The floor was a concrete slab, and in addition to the white-faced goat who greeted us at the door, there was a black baby goat who skittered in and out of the porch area when anybody opened the door and he could squeeze through. Along a ledge which ran halfway up the screen were bits of fossil and bone, rock crystals, and rusty hand tools.

She had been expecting us and had cooked a large pot of beans and a skillet of cornbread. She disappeared in and out of the main house setting utensils, plates, and food on the table for us. At her direction, we didn't try to follow her into this forbidden part of the house but sat on the beds watching both her and the goats as they tagged behind her. Then we ate and talked, getting acquainted with each other for the next several hours. Outside, the girls ran through the goat pens, petting the goats, laughing when they butted up against them playfully. Mrs. Babb cautioned them about going too far from the clearing, as the snakes were out and could be dangerous. But the girls were content to stay within the confines of the yard where the goats and chickens were.

When I asked to use the bathroom, Mrs. Babb pointed me out the screen door to the privy at the back part of the clearing. The door didn't close completely but was faced away from the house, so that it seemed private since there wasn't anyone looking for the next hundred miles facing front. When I came back onto the porch, Mrs. Babb asked me what I thought of its view. "I think you can't find a better view anywhere in the world than the one I have from my johnny!" I agreed that she should indeed be proud of her facility.

Later, she took us on a tour of the premises, proud of her goats, calling them by name. Chickens were busy pecking in and out of the pens. She told us that they roosted with the goats at night, so that she didn't have to worry about the hoot owls or coyotes getting to them. The pens were made of various materials: pieces of tin, sotol sticks bundled together, lengths of baling wire, chicken mesh, railroad ties, even large stones. They unfolded one into another, some open and large holding several goats, others small and enclosed. Two of the sheds I peered into, no larger than refrigerator crates, held mother goats, one with a sweet-faced brown kid, which Mrs. Babb told us was less than a day old. She listed off the exotic names: Angoras, Nubians, Alpines, Toggenbergs, Saanens. Some nudged us when we walked through, others stood aloof, legs apart, and still others shyly backed away. She cautioned us not to let them nibble on our shirts or pants. Her own hems were frayed and shredded at the edges, partially eaten away. By the time we returned to the house, a crowd of a dozen or more had gathered and continued to peer in at us on the porch as we talked the rest of the afternoon.

That day, Mrs. Babb talked to us at length about the hot springs not far from her house and what they could do for people. She expressed a sadness that the springs weren't being learned about by more people and hoped that Eleanor and I would at least go down to see them. She took off Eleanor's shoes and began to massage her feet. Then, after several minutes of massaging each toe and along each side to the ankle, she began massaging gently up and down Eleanor's arms, sides, and legs as she was talking—Eleanor had been complaining of general fatigue and pains in her lower back. After almost twenty minutes of massage, Mrs. Babb released her. Eleanor stretched out full across one of the beds, to indicate her complete relaxation.

We left just at sunset. The western sky was turning orange, bleeding red into Mrs. Babb's clearing as we pulled away, promising her we would come again soon. She waved and shaded her eyes to watch us as we drove slowly down the ridge. Long before we were out of the desert, it was completely dark, but Eleanor knew the roads well enough not to lose the way. As the stars began to appear, Eleanor told me that we were driving through a canyon area where red lights sometimes bobbed mysteriously across the face of the canyon walls and hopped across the desert floor. She said that Mrs. Babb can tell of having seen them many times and that once she herself saw them behind her coming along the very road we were on. She had thought at first they were approaching headlights, but then they had suddenly disappeared where there was no house or possible exit. In the backseat, the girls pricked up their ears. As we drove farther, they began to squeal and point.

"It's them!"

"I saw one!"

"Me too! Me too!"

I admit that I scrutinized the canyon walls myself. I was not sure of the red lights' reality, but if they were out there, I wanted to see them.

The children kept a sharp eye out for the mystery lights all the way. I never saw anything except uninterrupted darkness. Soon the car bumped, and there was black asphalt beneath us again. Lights began to appear on both sides of the road, farmhouses with the porch lights on, living room lights, and the lights of television. Another turn and we saw Sierra Blanca, a cluster of lights, with the long straight highway leading out of it. Once we were on the highway, the desert receded completely away into the darkness, and there was nothing but ourselves talking to each other, headed for El Paso, our headlights bobbing straight ahead on the road.

CHAPTER 2

Early Childhood

Narrated by Jewel Babb

I WAS BORN in Juno, Texas, August 13, 1900, but my mother and father only stayed there long enough to have me, and I don't remember the town. What I do remember as a child was taking long trips in the wagon. My daddy and my grandpa were professional well drillers, and they moved from one place to another. And the family—my grandpa and grandma and father and mother and myself—moved from one place to another in a covered wagon. My daddy drilled those water wells around Sheffield and Ozona. And it's on record up there, that he drilled those wells. And mother said they'd go down so deep, and they'd find an old pile of oil. But they didn't know what that was back then.

My daddy would stop for dinner in a place where there was plenty of grass for the livestock and horses. Of course he hobbled them so they couldn't get away. He'd just tie their feet together. While he was unhitching the horses, the rest of us would gather wood to make a fire to boil coffee and make the noon meal. It didn't make any difference if the weather was hot or cold, my mother cooked outside on a campfire. We would rest an hour or so, then hitch up the horses again to the wagon. Everything had to be packed again in the wagon. A keg with water for our use was wrapped in some kind of rags or sacks and tied onto the back of the wagon so that it was never hard to get a drink as needed. And the water was always cold. Then we'd start again and ride for about four hours. My daddy or grandpa would always be on the watchout for some level valley with grass enough for horses. A good place to camp for the night. He would always camp on a higher place, as he said, should a rain come during the night; we would be safer than if we had our camp in a low place.[1] Of course, as soon as he decided on a place to camp, momma began getting supper, had to get all unloaded again. Dishes, pots, and food to be prepared while the others began gathering wood here and there for the night. It took quite a bit. And then beds to be made before night on the ground around the wagon. Next morning when I got up, there was a big fire going, and everyone standing around the fire. Momma cooking breakfast and some drinking coffee. A beautiful sight that I never forgot. All my life I've loved a campfire and liked to cook over one.

Then after a good many days, we'd get to where my daddy and grandpa were going to drill another well. Then the permanent camp would be set up. Maybe it takened a month on one well. And my daddy was talented in many ways. He could tan hides and all, you see. So we'd go to a place where he was going to drill. So then before he started with the drilling, he cleared off a place for the tent. We always had a tent in the wagon, and then we had a little stove, a little four-burner stove just about knee-high. And my daddy, ever time he killed a pretty hide—a goat hide or a sheep hide—he tanned it. Then he'd square them off and stretch them, and then he takened buckskin and sewed the hides together. And some of that old sheep hide was thick, just about four or five inches when they had a year's growth of hair. And those were the prettiest things. I still remember it. Anyway, he'd clear a space off for the tent. Then he'd open tow sacks, and he'd take little wooden pegs, and he'd drive the pegs into the tow sacks spread out, and he'd tack them all down over this whole area. And then we had these iron beds, and he'd fix the iron beds up in there and the little stove and then put these rugs all over the floor. Oh, that was the warmest place! And if it was hot weather, we had a square piece of canvas for a porch, a "fly" they called it. And we'd stay in a place til he was through drilling, a month, maybe two.

We didn't have any recreation. I don't believe we even had books to read. But we were happy and contented. My parents did not play cards nor was any dominoes around. We just sat around the fire. People talked. Then we all went to bed. To this day, I do not play cards or know a thing about dominoes. Grandma would not allow them on the place. She would probably have thrown them in the fire.

After going to bed, the night birds would sing, mockingbirds and the whippoorwills, and I could heard the tinkling of the bells on the horses grazing. Altogether the most beautiful music in the world. I would go to sleep hearing them sing and the bells ringing. Then of course a coyote or a fox now and then. But I was not afraid of them, even though they'd get pretty close to camp sometimes. A lovely free world. That's the reason my parents had such a time keeping me in school. There were not many fences. Cattle guards were unheard of. Fences were miles apart and no one to tell you to move on. Maybe I was five on my last trip in a wagon going to and from drilling wells.

We always had clean, nice bedding, as my grandma loved to make quilts. We did not have money to buy material for quilts, neither the cotton or wool for padding, but every old gunny sack was washed, folded, and put away and used as the padding for inside of the quilt in the place of wool or cotton. Then she saved every back of a shirt, old dresses, the parts that wasn't worn. She'd piece all this together by hand for the top and bottom of the quilt. Then she would tack or quilt it with the twine she had unraveled from sacks. And when she'd finished it, we'd have a nice clean warm cover for the cold nights to come. My daddy or grandpa never left anywhere in the wagon without a nice bedroll. Of course, these quilts are a little heavy, but they are warm, too.

But I don't think my momma was real happy. Because she was like her mother, my Grandmother Bosworth. Her family had just roamed all over the country in a covered wagon. Momma says when her mother married, her husband helped her up in that wagon and she traveled with him for the next twenty-two years, just going here and yonder. All her children were born in that covered wagon. And she carried a feather bed with her all the time. And every time they come to a river, she'd get out her big tub, fill it with water and heat it, and everything in that wagon had to be scrubbed out. She was a fanatic when it come to cleaning. They say that wagon was as clean as could be.

Her husband—my Grandpa Bosworth—wasn't no good, kind of lazy like. He would move somewhere to get a job, but then if anybody moved close to him, he thought he was hemmed in. So he'd have to go look for another country that wasn't so crowded. He'd do any kind of work, but just for a few days. Then he'd get that wagon ready again and they'd move to another country. They moved all over this lower part of the country, backward and forward. One time when his oldest son got a pretty good size, close to Kerrville I guess, down in there somewheres, the boy come in one day and says, "There's some land over here for sale, maybe fifty cents an acre, maybe a dollar."

So my grandpa says, "Well, I'm not going to buy it, because in another fifty years it'll be the same price." Now no telling how much it's selling for.

So grandma never had a home. She had seven children. And grandpa didn't provide for her real well like my own daddy did us. But she'd keep house and cook over the fire. They said when she made coffee, she'd put the coffee in the pot, and when it was drunk up, then she'd put some more water on top of the other grounds in the morning and boil it and they'd drink that. Cause you know coffee was hard to get. Grandma and Grandpa Bosworth. And she was English. And grandma, she may have never owned a house, but whatever place she went to was spotless. And later on, I never liked to go see her because everything was so clean, so that I was afraid to walk anywhere, afraid that I might cause a wrinkle. She starched and ironed sheets, pillowcases, and tablecloths. I never knew where to sit. And she was always on the lookout for chinch bugs. She'd take the mattress out, let it sun, and look to see if there were chinch bugs, then throw boiling water on the bedframe, lye soap and water. They'd get in the walls and come out at night. And my poor mother, she was clean, too. She was a fanatic about her house just like her own mother. When I was still a child, grandma was living in Ozona. My uncle—her oldest son—bought her a little place there. She had a little house and all around it was rocks, just solid rocks all the way around it. Then she'd get out there and sweep those rocks off. And here I don't even sweep the house!

She started living there after the oldest boys got grown. She quit my grandfather. He had done with living in this Texas country, and he said it was crowded and that he was going to New Mexico. But on the state line, she said, "Woody, I'm not going."

So he got mad, got on his horse and taken off. So the two oldest boys were big enough to help her. So they hitched up the wagon and turned back. And then my grandpa wandered just here and yon and finally he came to Big Bend. He was killed in a cave down in Mexico, and they always said Pancho Villa and his men killed him. They thought he was looking for a treasure. But Grandmother Bosworth couldn't rest even after death. When the big flood came in Sanderson, her grave got washed away.

But my daddy's mother, Grandma Wilson, was just like me. She mostly wanted to have plenty of bedding and the house didn't have to be too clean. Grandma Wilson came from Tennessee when she was a child. She was part Indian and I tell you, she was a smart woman. She knew how to cure with all kinds of herbs. I imagine she was a fourth Indian, but I don't know what kind. Lucindy Belle Starr. She was a little old tiny thing, with black hair and blue eyes.

She was an awful pretty woman. I didn't have much sense, but I'd listen to her.

When they came from Tennessee through Indian territory, they went through at night and wrapped the wagon wheels in some kind of cloth so they wouldn't make a noise. And they settled in Starr County close to Pandale.

My grandpa was a big man, mostly Irish, I guess. But they must have met each other here in Texas. And where she came from, the Indians had come to the door of her house, called her daddy out, and him and her two brothers were killed right there at the door. I think that must have happened in Tennessee. They didn't bother the women folks, and maybe some of the other men were hiding inside. But those three, they just hauled off and killed them. Shot them.

But she had one great fear. She was deathly afraid of storms. They had to build her a dugout in Del Rio after we settled down there, a little room underground big enough for the whole family. They had to put a bed in it, lamp, food, water, and axe. And any big clouds she saw coming up, we would go to the dugout right quick. It was a little dangerous in the summertime, as the centipedes and scorpions went into it, too, though I've never seen a snake in one. Since there were lots of thunderstorms, we lived underground about a fourth of the time. My oldest son, too, he got that streak. When he came out in this part of the country, he had some Mexicans to dig a big hole; then he put a station wagon in it for a dugout. In case of a tornado. He never did see one, but he had that streak.

Grandma knew a lot about sick people, but she didn't like the well people, didn't get along with them. When a person was sick, the first thing she done was get a big pan of hot water and let them soak their feet in hot water. So you see, that kind of work with water and working on the feet goes back quite a ways. Soaking your feet will stop a headache. My grandma wasn't religious, but my momma was. Grandma just didn't believe in all that. But she sure helped the sick people. Grandma lived til she was ninety-two. Daddy died before she did.

My momma didn't have that much to do with me. It was my Grandma and Grandpa Wilson that I liked the best. And I didn't have to do much work. I played. Run off out here and they always had a hard time with me, because each animal that came up to the tent, where I could see them, I'd follow them off. So they had to watch me. Then I'd be playing outside all the time, and every bug or grasshopper, anything I could get, I would take back into the tent and put in my bed. So at nighttime, they had to go check my bed every time and see what was in it.

My brother, Hollie, and I didn't have any toys, only what was called then a Barlow knife. I hated dolls, and Christmas, my parents bought us each a pocket knife. But there were lizards and butterflies to be chased, birds' nests to be looked into if they were low enough, baby birds with their little mouths wide open, ready to eat the worms, grasshoppers, and other insects their mothers and fathers brought them. There were stick horses from sotol stalks. My grandfather would tie strings around the big end of them for reins to keep the pony in line, and we raced around the tent and, later on, the house. My grandfather would take his knife and cut all the rough spots off of these sticks, and our horses would be a pretty yellow or white.

Then if Hollie and I wandered a ways from our camp, we might find where an old cow had died, and her horns were lying around. We were always glad to find a horn. We takened them back to the camp, got a piece of glass that our parents had picked up somewhere, set down in the shade, and spent many hours scraping these horns. It might take several days of work on one horn. Then when my grandfather looked at it and thought it was ready, he sawed off the sharp point of the horn and, with a red hot wire, he would burn a hole through the small part of the horn until it went through into the hollow of the horn. Then we had a horn that we could blow on. And it would make a noise!

Then there were old horse shoes that we could play with, too. We set on the ground and dug holes in the dirt with them. Sometimes there would be a big fat frog to be watched. And little ground squirrels, running into their holes in the ground. Once we tried to drown them out. We carried all the water we could and poured in their holes, and in a minute they crawled out. But it didn't take us long to find out they had the sharpest teeth. There were big fat grasshoppers to be killed, pulled apart, and takened to a near bird's nest and dropped into the open mouth of a tiny bird. Seemed the birds didn't know the difference. And there were so many birds, scissortails, mocking birds, and sometimes a blue-and-red bird I did not know. There was also the night birds, whippoorwills, calling in the evening with many more.

One bird that we always tried to keep away from was the killdeer, or kill-dee as we called them. If we got near their rock-looking eggs on the ground, they were always watching from close by, and when they saw a chance, they'd fly back to their open nest on the ground, grab an egg, or one of their babies, in their mouth, fly off a ways and drop the egg or baby. Of course then the eggs would be broken. And the young killed.

I don't remember seeing very many rattlesnakes or copperheads when I was a child. And I do not know of very many times we were told to watch out for snakes. I reckon momma watched us, but from a distance. And I do remember hearing about a young boy who was sickly back then. He put his hand in a can, and there was a snake in it that bit him. The venom killed his disease, and he was supposed to have been well after that. The venom, I've been told, seems to cure everything in the system if you're sick.

And, too, after a rain or shower there were tiny tan or brown baby frogs, hopping everywhere. We would get an old can or bucket and catch dozens and play with them for hours. Of course soon they all died. Sometimes grandma would say they came with the rain. But who knows? Maybe they were in the ground somewhere and they only came out when it rained.

Then at night when we went to bed, there were crickets. They began singing at dark. They seemed to be everywhere. And along with all the songs of the night birds, we would go to sleep listening to all of this wonderful music. Then long toward morning, something would wake us up walking around on top of the house or the tent, and we would be scared until it would go, "hoo! hoo!" Then we knew it was only a big hoot owl.

Many hours we would set and whittle on a soft sotol stick. We would try to make different things with our knives. Seems at all times, we were contented with the few things we had and was happy.

One time grandpa bought a little ranch below Brackettville. The wagon was loaded and we started out. It was not very much of a trip, but as we got close to the little house, I can still see the big oak trees we had to go under before getting to the ranch. They were high, and streamers of big grey moss hung down. Once in a while, a big old hoot owl would get scared and fly away out of the big trees. They always made cold chills run up and down my back. There were so many, always hoo, hoo, even setting on top of the house waking you up in the midnight hours and early morning.

When we were in the live oak country, Hollie and I would go out where there were big old oak trees with their long ghostly mosses. We'd get in a shady spot, lay down on our backs, and for hours watch the squirrels, hawks, and birds move about in the great tree tops where they had their homes. The prettiest of all were the big red squirrels, darting here and there looking down at us mostly from behind limbs or clumps of leaves with their bright shiny black eyes.

There were armadillos, too, with their steel-like shells. We could chase them into their holes. Then we would get them by the tail, and we'd pull and pull. Then we'd try to dig them out. But we couldn't. If we ever caught one and a pond of water was near, we'd both carry the armadillo to the water and throw him in. He would disappear. But after watching a good while, he'd crawl out on the other side from us. Seems he walked on the muddy bottom clear across from us.

There were also turtles we'd find walking around. Some had pretty stripes and designs on the top of their shells. Also, their under-shell would be pretty. You could not get much action from them, as they'd go back into their house, or shell, and be real quiet, as if they were dead.

Sometimes, if we sat still for a long time, a bunch of musk hogs would come out in the opening and graze along eating roots and plants. They are a strange animal. They make good watch dogs and will run with a pack of dogs. And they're always ready to fight a stranger if one comes up to the house. A peccary.

We'd find a nest of rabbits sometimes. We'd take them home and grandma would help us fix a box and bed for them. But we could only raise the jackrabbits. A cotton tail is never as tame as a jackrabbit. But most all the time, the rabbits would get out of their box and disappear, maybe with our parents' help.

And in the springtime. So many flowers of all colors. Growing together. Black-eyed Susans and the other yellow-and-dark brown flowers. They called them "nigger-toes." Redbud trees everywhere, on top of the little hills and in the valleys. Mountain laurel with their purple clusters of bloom. Their waxy green leaves were beautiful, although we were told not to gather the flowers, as they were poison.[2] Then, above all the flowers we liked the best was the Indian paintbrush. They were a dark peach or light rust color. The flowers grew on the tall stems, and the whole plant together formed a cluster. We would always gather an armful of all the flowers and take them back to grandma or momma. Grandma would look at the lovely Indian paintbrushes. Then she would tell us of her early days when she was growing up among the Indians in Tennessee.

My parents never fought or quarreled in front of us children. That way we were never upset or unhappy. After we were settled there in this new place, we were very happy. We had a big fireplace and lots of good oak wood. My grandparents were early risers and would get up at daybreak to milk the cows. I wanted to milk the cows, too, and no way could they slip out to the pen without me. My grandpa would start building a fire in the fireplace. I'd be right there, too, getting so close—it was winter—that I'd get into the ashes. But when grandpa went to the pens to milk, I was right with him when he was milking. I'd reach under his hand and try to milk one tit, too. He never scolded or told me to go away. I don't remember how old I was when I learned to milk. The only time I was told to go away was in the kitchen. Momma and daddy cooked. Grandma and grandpa were good cooks, too, so they always said I'd waste something or get in the way, and I got out.

Everybody went to a little dance now and then, just a few ranchers. Everyone would take something to eat, as the dance would last all night. And the musicians—violin and guitar—could play only a few tunes. They were played over and over all night.

Momma was also running the switchboard at Laguna then. I would be so tickled if she would be out for a minute. I'd answer the phone and they'd say, "Is this Mrs. Wilson?" And I'd say, "Yes." I don't reckon I was over six. Nothing pleased me better than trying to answer the phone.

I don't know how long we stayed at this place. It seems my parents sold it just a short while after moving to it. Then they bought or leased another small place, and it was more isolated. Beyond Silver Lake on the other side of Brackettville. The lake was so pretty. But when we moved to this little place, it was the worst place of all. An old, old house with trees and brush all around it. Some vegetation nearly growing in the house. I don't know how they ever cleaned up a place like that. Briars, vegetation, trees everywhere, so thick in places you could not get through. Then they bought 150 head of Spanish goats. My brother and I were to herd them. I could not have been over eight, and Hollie was two years younger. Anyway, we did herd these goats. They must have been gentle, as we had no trouble. We'd start out in the morning and didn't come back until evening. We did not have any shoes, even though it was very rough—rocks and thorns and such. Our feet soon became used to it. Even running on the rough ground didn't hurt our feet. And I know now that going barefoot helps you keep the points circulating.[3] The main thing I remember is we would be in the high trees and brush and couldn't see much. Then we would go on a ways up over a hill, look down below us, and see the prettiest little thicket of wild plums. The fruit would be bright orange and red. The little plum trees would be full of this fruit. We'd spend a while gathering some to take back to the ranch, as momma made good jelly. And we'd eat the sweetest ones.

One evening a panther followed us back home. We always had a little dog with us. This night after dark, the little dog barked. We didn't hear anything else from the dog. But in a minute or so, a panther screamed. Everybody was scared, and no one went outside. It was really dark. But next morning, the little dog was dead right at the back door. Seems they had a good pole pen and shed for goats, as they weren't hurt.

I loved to milk the goats, and I loved them just like I do these I have now. So I'd milk them, but momma would say, "Don't you bring that goat milk in the house. It's dirty." And I was so sad. My grandma said, "Well, it was all right," but momma: "No, not in the house."

We never lacked for something green to eat. My grandma and grandpa would go out in the pasture on one side of the road and gather pursley.[4] It has a little round leaf, and you boil it, then take it out of the water and fry it just a little bit in hot grease. They also gathered careless weed,[5] which you cook the same way, and wild peppers. We'd use them for seasoning. And for a good medicine tea, grandma would make it out of the horehound weed.[6] That tea was horrible beyond description, the worst taste that ever was. Most always the big can of homemade hominy was kept on back of the wood stove made with oak wood ashes. They'd fry a lot of homemade salt pork, then take the pork out of the pan, dip a lot of hominy out of the big can into the skillet, and let it simmer. They knew what was good! In those days we had plenty to eat.

This is the way I learned to make hominy. First thing to do is to get a big old iron pot. Then take a fourth of a sack of corn and have a great big tarp or some other cover on the ground. Then take this corn, hold it way up high when the wind is blowing. Way up high. And just let it drop, drop out a little. And the wind will blow off the husks and different little parts of it, you see, the little kernels that aren't very strong. So you do that two or three times til you get every bit of trash blown off. Then when it is clean, you just empty it into this pot that is full of water and ashes. That's what we used before we used lime. Then cook it and cook it, keep stirring it so it doesn't burn, and cook it til the husks begin to turn loose. Then pour all that stuff off, ashes and everything. Then wash it and wash it til it is clean, til the eyes come off, real clean and white looking. Then put it in some fresh clean water and boil it til it gets fat. Then take it in a big forty-eight–pound lard can and put it on the back of the stove. And every time momma cooked anything, she had a big dipper. She'd dip in there and cook it up in grease. And that's the best stuff you ever saw.

Momma made tomato pudding, too, but I don't like it. I won't eat it. But this other pudding made out of sourdough bread, oh, I never forgot how good it was—like a bread pudding. The old biscuits would get hard, as she saved everything. Then she'd wait until she had a big bunch of bread—the hard bread. Then she'd soak it in sweet milk, add butter and sugar, and that's about all. Then she'd bake it. But that tomato pudding, I never wanted to find out how she made it. I never learned how to cook til I married, til I was sixteen. My grandmother would say—we was poor people—"Now you get out of here or you might waste something." So I never learned.

We also had to make our own candles, because way out in the country you couldn't keep coal oil. There was nothing else for light. So grandma would take sacks, the ones you can use for strings. She would unravel the tops and keep all of those strings. So she'd twist all of those strings together. Then she'd have some taller[7] that she'd kept. She'd take this taller and melt it and then she'd dip the string in this hot grease, hold it up, and let it harden. And then she'd dip it again, and directly it got big. Then if we didn't have a candle, we'd take a pot of hot grease and twist a rag and put it in the grease. There'd be just a little piece of rag sticking up over the edge, and we used that for light, too. I've done this myself, after I was married. Because a lot of times we didn't have coal oil or anything like that.

And then for making soap we saved all the grease from the meat and rendered it up. Then we put it in buckets and put it away. To make soap, we had some lye. We'd put the lye and the grease in a big pot, then stirred it and stirred it. So. That was our soap. And then we'd have a big washing. So after washing, we'd take the water and scrub the floors with it. It was good soap, though.

Finally, after a few months, I guess grandpa and daddy sold the goats and moved to Brackettville. They put me in school there, but I don't know how long we stayed. Then we moved to Del Rio, this time to stay. We bought a bigger old house, six rooms, and a porch back and front. And I started to school again. I did fairly well in history, reading, spelling, and writing, but arithmetic was just not for me in no grade. My parents had to follow me to school, because every time they'd turn back and there was a house between me and the school, I'd set down and wouldn't go on. I hated it! If you're loose all the time, you know, and have freedom, then you don't want to be penned up. So I played hookey most of the time. They had a time keeping me in school. Most all the time, I had a girl friend and both of us would just walk down to the draw and look around for birds' nests, or go to the cemetery and look at all the graves.

But I kept on til I had finished the sixth and that was it. I stopped when I was about fourteen years old. One time I was writing free-hand, and I started writing backhand, and the teacher got on me for that. Still, I can't write all my letters in the same direction. I mix them up. So I was a sixth-grade dropout. Well, now, my brother did graduate and started work with Convair. And at first he was a floor sweeper. But in twenty-two years, he worked up to missile inspector. "So you know," he told me, "you really don't have to go to school if you'll read books." He said that with books you can educate yourself. You set down here and study one chapter, and then you go back the next day and it's there again. You don't have to depend on a teacher telling you. I think the important thing is if you want to know. So I gave up on school when I was about fourteen. No, I didn't give up, my parents gave up on me. I'd given up a long time before. Schooling just wasn't for me. But my parents didn't worry about me that much, not in those days. A woman, see, wasn't counted as much.

CHAPTER 3

Healing with the Mind

WHEN I FIRST thought of doing a book with Mrs. Babb, she was still living at the tie house. Through a series of letters, we had agreed that I would stay with her for a period of time, perhaps three months in all, and help her out with chores and with the goats, in addition to transcribing the story of her life. But then I received bad news. She had taken a bad fall at the tie house, had hit her head, and was not feeling very well. Shortly thereafter, she moved to Valentine, Texas.

After she was settled in, however, we took up our plans again, and in January of 1977 I made my first trip out to be with her. I planned the first time to stay for a week. My husband, Chuck, was on winter break from the university and decided to spend this time with us, as he was ready for a change from academics and paper grading. Eleanor agreed to look after my children during the project. Chuck and I collected together the usual offering—peanut butter, graham crackers, coffee, and bread—and made the drive in our Volkswagon, going through Sierra Blanca this time, turning south at Van Horn.

Valentine is on the Southern Pacific railroad line. A town of two hundred, it is slowly losing its population because the railroad no longer needs the station for refueling, since the engines have switched to diesel fuel. Mrs. Babb's house was located on a dirt road running parallel to the railroad tracks. There was a scattering of other small houses along the road, and in back of her house was desert rolling flat, building up to the high Saw Tooth Mountains and Mount Livermore. I say desert, but the terrain was different here from what I had found in the Sierra Blanca region. Even then, in the dead of winter, it was apparent that it was high plains area, as dead grass stood knee high, interspersed with greasewood and cactus. We pulled up into a cleared area by the side of the house, which was a low adobe structure, somewhat weather-beaten but in better shape than most of the other houses we had passed on the road. In back of the house were goat sheds and in the front yard a pack of small dogs, which yapped at us incessantly as we walked to the door.

Mrs. Babb was fixing lunch when we came in. She called to us to come through the living room to the kitchen in the back of the house. When we came through the door, she wiped her hands on a dish towel and gave me a hug. She knew in advance that I would be bringing my husband on this trip, so she greeted him by name, extending her hand to be shaken.

Her stove was beside the kitchen window in the back of the house so that she could look out at her goats while she was cooking. She had kept sixteen of them—the old ones that she loved and couldn't give away and young ones that she wanted to see grow up a little more, the best of the milkers and the sweetest of the tempers. Lunch that day was barbeque links cooked with pieces of pork in sauce, grease gravy (grease, milk, flour, salt, and pepper), bread, butter, homemade apple preserves, instant coffee. Mrs. Babb has never claimed to be a cook, but her meals were always good and plentiful. While she was in the kitchen, there was an insistent bump against the back door.

"You go on now, Lena. I'll be out for you later," she called out, stirring the gravy. She confided to us that this was the oldest and most spoiled of the goats. She wasn't kept in the goat pen with the others but had been given the run of the yard and occasional entrance to the kitchen.

Over lunch, Mrs. Babb told us that she didn't like staying in Valentine and was missing the solitude of the tie house and the desert around it. She was leery of the so-called conveniences of this town house. There was water, for instance, piped into the house, although there was no hot water heater. The pipes were somehow faulty and leaking, and she was having a hard time getting anyone in the town to fix them, as there were no skilled laborers in Valentine. In the evening, she turned the water off completely but would give us a bucket for our room in case we needed to relieve ourselves during the night. But there was electricity in the house, and a gas heater in the front room which kept the room warm in the winter if she wanted to use the butane, which she found expensive. While company was at the house, that was usually what she used. But when she was by herself (and later when she and I were alone together), she used a wood-burning stove in a small room off the dining room, as she could easily gather sticks and scraps of twigs and branches in the plains on the outskirts of the town to feed the fire, and the little room stayed comfortably warm from the heat of the stove alone.

That afternoon, I helped with the goats for the first time. We threw two leaves of alfalfa into the pen. All the goats flocked around but the two oldest ones. She fed them separately because the young ones wouldn't let them eat. While the others went after the alfalfa, she slipped the old ones out of the pen and fed them horse and mule feed (corn, grain, and pellets) by the back porch.

Grisella was the largest goat. She was black with long horns, had golden eyes, and looked very wise, but was quite bossy. Later, Mrs. Babb brought out horse and mule feed for everyone. She put it on pieces of tin in the goat yard. Grisella butted everyone else off the piece of tin she was eating from. Some of the goats ate kneeling on their front knees. They carefully lowered themselves down and cleaned up everything within reach. There was a white rooster who ate the feed, too, anything scattered away from the tin. He waded right into the middle of the goats, with them butting and pawing each other for the best morsels. But he didn't blink an eye, striding among them with complete aplomb. There were no billy goats. Mrs. Babb said there would be too many kids and they would come at the wrong time, which was hard on the females and kids both, having babies in the winter.

The rest of the day, with only a short break for leftovers at suppertime, we gathered around the heater in the front room. Mrs. Babb sat in an old chair by the window, and we sat on the couch, drinking coffee and looking at photographs from her childhood. She was moving more slowly than when I had visited with her at the tie house, but she still became animated with attention. Her voice was husky and musical with a slight catch. She said that she once had a broken blood vessel in her esophagus which caused her voice to waver, but to my ear it sounded very similar to the melodic waver the goats speak with to each other.

A little after eight-thirty, she began to signal that she was tired. She showed us our room, a small front bedroom off the living room. One thing she said that she did like about the house was that she had so much room to sleep people in. Every room, including the living room, had its iron bedstead piled high with handmade quilts.

"I have a name for having the best beds," she told us. "Now I don't keep them so good, but I used to."

Our bed looked extremely well kept to me. It was piled high with a feather comfort and mohair blankets: mohair, she said, because she liked goats so much. She was obviously proud of the bed she had made for us and pointed out how easy it would be for us to slip under the covers and read for a little while (the room was not heated and was much colder than the living room). After she said good-night, we did just that. Then after Chuck put the light out a little later, we sank down into the bed for easy sleeping, wrapped in feathers carefully chosen and put together for maximum comfort.

This continued to be the pattern of the days spent with Mrs. Babb. Generally I would type in the mornings; then in the afternoons we would talk together and do general chores. Mrs. Babb loved to tell anecdotes about her various animals, indicating that she had spent a good deal of time observing their behavior and talked directly to them much as she talked with people. One of the most entertaining histories was the one she gave for the large white rooster in her backyard whose job it was to guard the goats. When I had gone out into the backyard by myself the first time, he paced the fence between the goats and me, stretching his neck and crowing. He followed every move I made and tried to herd me either back into the house or around to the front yard. He never came to trust me while I was there, always sure that I was after his goats. Mrs. Babb said he was raised out at the tie house with the goats. When she moved to Valentine, he went across the street with the other chickens in the roost of one of her nephews who lived in a small house there. The nephew had goats, too. But Mrs. Babb said it didn't take the rooster long to realize that those goats weren't his. So he began crossing the street every morning so that he could spend the day with his goats. And every afternoon, he would go back home. Finally, he realized there was enough room for him to roost with his own goats, and he just moved in.

In addition to our general talk, Mrs. Babb gave Chuck two treatment sessions the first week we were there. He had had hepatitis only a few months before, and his liver had been damaged, causing him discomfort and indigestion. The first treatment was given at twilight, and the only light in the room came from the gray square of the window and the gaslight of the heater. Mrs. Babb sat in her big armchair by the window with her palms held up toward Chuck, who was sitting, relaxed, on the couch. She still had hay in her hair from the last feeding time of the goats at sunset. The room was very quiet and peaceful. I sat on the couch by Chuck and remained quiet throughout the session.

She asked him to report what he was feeling. He said that there was a pain when she first started, but then it went away. He said he felt a pressure that was moving, that it felt very good, as if there were a hand in the area of the liver, pressing.

She said, "There is!" She told him she could "see" a hump on the liver, a swelling out or a lump. He said he felt a slight pain again in his side and that the pain seemed to be spreading. They sat for about fifteen minutes, exchanging information like this, Chuck with his head bowed and his eyes closed, reporting the sensations he apparently felt from time to time. The only sound in the room other than these exchanges was the hiss from the gas heater. It was so relaxing that I was almost asleep. Finally, Mrs. Babb lowered her hands. She told Chuck she would give him another treatment in the morning, which would include a foot massage and some work on his back.

Mrs. Babb claims healing power from "seeing" the affected area of the patient's body. To illustrate what she meant by this, she recounted the story of an El Paso man, Don W., who was bitten by a black widow spider while foraging for herbs in the desert. He came to Mrs. Babb's tie house and stayed with her, receiving treatment. She could "see" little black spots in his bloodstream. Even after he left the house, she could "see" him all the way to Ysleta, the black dots dispersing gradually, and knew he was going to be all right.

During a treatment, she holds her hands out, palms toward the patient. She says a sensation of warmth starts in one of her hands, then arcs to the other, and that the energy and warmth seem to circulate in the palms. Sometimes this energy can become so intense in her hands that she says it can cause her discomfort and at times even get out of control. She recounted one incident of this occurring:

"I went to see a Mexican man one time across the river and worked with him. The sensation of heat got into my hands. I was at his place and not mine, and I hadn't ever been in his place before. A little old place by the river. So the heat got to be too much in my hands, and I bathed in cold water. The heat was at my elbows then I went back to the tie house. By then, it was into my chest and abdomen, but when I entered my place, it vanished. I think it was the good spirits of the place from all my praying. That drove it away. God has protected me like that all my life. But that'll happen. You can go to a beer joint or bad dance hall, pick up those evil energies, and take them home with you."[1]

After the treatment was over for the evening, she lectured us on the necessity of preventive medicine for liver problems.

"Haven't you read about way back in Arkansas where they had poke salad and everything, and when it was growed up, ripe and ready, they used it to clean the liver and the system. Course I've used poke salad[2]—fried up in grease like spinach. But I think it's better than spinach. So if the liver's not taken care of, it gets full of poison. Then it can't work. And then the gall bladder. I think it must have something to do with the gall bladder, cause if the gall bladder don't secrete its little juices in the stomach, you can't digest nothing. And then that makes rocks, also."[3]

I asked her: "So there are several things you can use to clean the liver?"

"Yes," she replied. "Long years ago, I think they used sassafras.[4] Cascara.[5] And first thing I can remember is calomel,[6] and I mean, when you take a dose of calomel, you think you're a goner! Then when we got more advanced, we had Black Draught,[7] and that was just as bad. That was the most horrible thing I've ever taken in my life. It was tea. We'd boil the leaves and make a hot tea. Yellow with black letters, packages of different leaves, different plants. And that was the awfullest thing you've ever saw in your life. And then finally, later on, we got to using Syrup of Pepsin[8] and everything else. Take about every two weeks, take a dose of it. Take a tablespoon.

"But poke salad in the springtime. Or horehound. That grows around here. You ever heard of that? That's good, too."

After Chuck and I went to bed, I asked him if he had, in fact, felt the sensations he had reported to her. He admitted that he had really felt something, and he described it as the sensation of little hands, several little hands, kneading and massaging. But he was quick to point out the difficulty of remaining objective under the circumstances.

A second treatment session occurred the next morning. Mrs. Babb first asked Chuck how he was feeling. He said there was quite a bit of pressure on his liver, that he felt "them" really pushing on the liver and felt "they" were going to finish up the job. As he said this, I looked closely into his face for signs of the put-on, but he was as matter-of-fact as Mrs. Babb was, both of them exchanging information as casually as if they were talking about the weather. We assumed the places we had occupied the night before, Mrs. Babb in the worn armchair by the window, holding her hands up and out toward Chuck to direct the healing energies. Nute, one of her grandchildren was still asleep on his pallet on the floor. Wayne Babb had dropped him off late the night before on the way out to run his traps. There was a gray sky outside, but the goat bells in the background relieved the gloominess. During the session, there was a train whistle, then a train bell, the sound of steam brakes being released, the screeching of wheels coming to a long stop.

Mrs. Babb said, "I start to go to work on the liver, but then they go to other places and work on that." She had said before that she was never in complete control, that "they" knew where to go and headed for the worst places. "It seems like that hump isn't so big," she said. "Well, we'll go to your back now." They sat again silently.

When I looked at Nute, his eyes were open and looking at me, although he hadn't moved beneath the covers. This kind of activity apparently was nothing new to him, and he expressed no interest in what was going on. He smiled, however, when he saw me looking at him.

Chuck began to report on his sensations. He said that the pressure was moving around in his body, first to one spot, then another. The sensation, he said, was a good one and felt very warm and comforting. Sometimes it climbed the spine, then made a triangle between the kidneys and a spot beneath them. In reply, Mrs. Babb told him to move his back around, to stand up and stretch. He did—standing up, then bending down, and standing up again. He demonstrated how the hands moved on his kidneys—"as if they were big enough to hold the whole thing." Then he sat back down and moved from one side to another. Mrs. Babb came over and put her hand on Chuck's side, which he had told her was stiff. She laid it there for about two minutes, then kneaded into his side, then turned him around and began to massage down his back. Her fingers were thick at the fingertips instead of tapering, giving her extra strength. She remarked casually as she massaged that the room was full of spirits and full of music— "You just need to turn on the right kind of radio to catch some of it." The sun had come out from its clouds, and the room was suddenly lit. It had been a remarkably peaceful and invigorating session, even for me, who had done nothing more than sit quietly for half an hour.

Later, I questioned her about the process of treating patients with the mind.

P.E.T.: "Do you ever have any idea how it's going to work?"

MRS. B: "No, I don't. I just wait and see what they're going to do."

P.E.T.: "Do you see any similarities—like, for instance, broken bones. Do they tend to act the same way, or is it all different?"

MRS. B: "I think that pus—infection—hurts the worst. But with other problems, like with broken bones, there's just heat or a tingling or something, and that's all."

P.E.T.: "A sensation of pressure like Chuck was feeling?"

MRS. B: "Yes. It's all just about alike."

P.E.T.: "Now, the person you're working on. He can be doing just practically anything during treatment? Talking or working—"

MRS. B: "Well, I like them just to kind of be quiet so I'll know what's going on. But I can talk. It doesn't matter."

P.E.T.: "But they need to tell you what they're feeling. Now you mentioned a man who just didn't have any belief at all. Does it take belief to heal?"

MRS. B: "No, doesn't make no difference. No, he needed to stay for more treatment, that's all. Sometimes it takes longer. But it does take something to heal somebody else. Only a good person can heal. God can't work through a person for healing unless she is a good person. A bad person has so many spiritual dark clouds around them that the light can't get to them."

P.E.T.: "Do you need to touch the person with your hands during the treatment process?"

MRS. B: "At first I thought I did. That was when I was finding out about how it all worked. There was one time back then that a car fell on top of Agustín. He couldn't get the jack to fit together right. So he finally got an old jack, and then it slipped. I had to find boards and stack them up to get the car off of him. Bolts had come into his ear and cut him badly. He couldn't walk because his hip was hurt. So I takened him up to the hospital in Van Horn. He was on the table shaking, and I put my hands on his head. The doctor told him he had a fractured pelvis and he'd be on crutches for a year. So he was in the hospital for ten or eleven days and had pain from the pelvis to the ribs. The doctor gave him pain killers and sent him home. But he was still in pain. But I put my hands on his head, and the pain went away. And he was off his crutches in three weeks. But now I know that I don't need the touching all the time. I could do him long distance if I'd known it, and he wouldn't have to wait that long."

P.E.T.: "Who have you done by long distance?"

MRS. B: "Well, there was a little girl in Oklahoma City, and she had a knot or lump in the lower stomach, and I worked with her. Looked like a light went along the back of her, and she said she felt something soothing. Then there was this woman who I worked with at the springs who had bursitis in her shoulder. I helped her take baths at the springs. So after a few days we stopped, and she came out to the tie house and stayed all night. And in the morning, she said, 'My shoulder hurt me last night.' So I said, 'Let's just give it a massage.' And so I just massaged this shoulder and reached all the way to the bone and pulled up, just all the way from the bone. So she went back home and got her leather machine. She was a seamstress. She had sold the machine because she hadn't been able to use that shoulder. So she bought the machine back and went back to sewing. And then in two years the other shoulder got bad. And she come to the springs again. But she said, 'I don't have the time to stay here.' But I said she didn't have to, that I could work on it while she was away. She said, 'Yes, by remote control.' And she said that when she come back home one night from work, something just got hold of that shoulder and massaged—deep massage. It felt like someone was really getting hold of her. And then it healed up."

P.E.T.: "And that wasn't necessarily when you were thinking about it. It wasn't necessarily at the same time—"

MRS. B: "That's right. I don't have to think about it all the time."[9]

That evening, Mrs. Babb gave me a general foot massage. Although I felt to be in good health, she uses the foot massage for diagnostic purposes as well as for treatment of specific illnesses, as, according to her, undue tenderness at any pressure point in the foot indicates a potential trouble spot.

She put one of my feet in her lap. I stretched out across her bed on my elbows, and she sat on the end, pressing and pulling, punching with a finger, pinching with a thumb and forefinger, up and down between the bones, into each joint, over and down and around each tendon and muscle. Her head was close to my foot, and her hands were very firmly on my leg so that her hold didn't falter, regardless of the starts and jerks I might make. There was something very delicious about this experience. It reminded me of being a very small child with my foot in my mother's lap and her fingers tweaking each toe: "This little piggy went to market . . ." And the stories my grandfather has told me of the foot-washing ceremonies he used to go to on Sunday, when men washed each other's feet.

From time to time, Mrs. Babb looked over my toes into my face: "How does this feel?" she said. "And this? And this? This here now is the gall bladder. And this 'un's the liver," naming the connections each pressure point is supposed to have as she moved from spot to spot. She exerted a great deal of pressure with her fingers on various points. Her thumbs were broad and her hands sinewy and strong. But there was no real pain involved. Primarily, I enjoyed it for the strength and comfort of her hands on my body. Soon she straightened up, giving my foot a pat, then started on the other.

"I'll say this, Pat," she told me after finishing my other foot, "I reckon you're pretty healthy." She said this because there had been no knots, no major areas of pain underneath her prodding which would have indicated a trouble area. I grinned at her and nodded my head like a four-year-old, delighted at the pronunciation of good health from this woman. Later, when I returned to El Paso, I found myself telling friends with a somewhat silly pride that Mrs. Babb said I was healthy, that I had the healthiest feet around.

CHAPTER 4

A Ranch Marriage

Narrated by Jewel Babb

I MARRIED when I was sixteen. I'd met Walter about four months before we married. He came from rich ranch people. Rich in land and stock. I was coming up this street in Del Rio, and I looked up in front of me, and I saw two boys coming, acting like they were drunk. Of course, they were laughing about something. Anyway, I just ducked into a little candy shop, and they came in, too. And that's where I met him. I lived in town, and he come in from that ranch to see me, and later in 1916 we got married. He was too bashful, and I was, too, so there wasn't much courting.

He'd come to see me on the train. Then if we wanted to go anywhere, we walked. My home was a good two miles from the main part of town. We married one evening, just the minister and a few friends. Then the next morning, he had to get on the train and go back to the ranch. I was to follow in a week. So when the time came, momma and daddy put me on the train to go meet him at Langtry—home of Judge Roy Bean. It was the first time I'd ridden on a train. When the train got to Langtry, I got right off in front of Judge Roy Bean's old saloon and office building.[1] There was Walter waiting for me. He was in some sort of old Model T. I got in the old thing, and we started out. It was just about like riding in a wagon. So rough! But we finally made it to the headquarters ranch and my new life.

A few weeks after I'd been at the ranch, roundup time started, and since the ranch was a big one—two hundred sections—the cowboys had to move from place to place. So since everyone was getting ready to go, I wanted to go, too. My father-in-law talked to me and said, "Women don't go on roundups with the men." But he finally promised to let me go.

But I had no clothes for such a trip. So my mother-in-law says,

"We will go get Lucy to make you a couple of riding skirts and some blouses." And since they always kept duckin' jackets on hand, she found one that fitted me and also some heavy blue denim cloth for the riding skirts. So in a few days Lucy, my sister-in-law, came with the two riding skirts and blouses. They fitted me to a T. Lucy was an expert at making riding clothes and made them for all the women of the family. When all was ready, my flour sack was tied on my saddle with all my belongings and extra clothes.

My riding skirts had big pockets on them. The skirt came below the calf of the leg. The pockets were big enough to carry a twenty-two pistol, which Walter and my grandpa said I must keep in my pocket at all times. My grandpa gave me his cherished forty-five—a "hog leg," as it was called. It was nearly too big for me to hold. I was more afraid of these pistols than I was of the many kinds of varmints and the different classes of men who always worked on the ranch. I was also to wear a bonnet at all times to keep the sun from burning my face and also to keep a pretty complexion. I wore heavy shoes. I never wore boots, as I did not like them. One thing I always kept handy was a jar of Pond's Cold Cream. I could never use water and soap on my face.

Walter didn't know that I wasn't a good rider, especially on these quick cow ponies. They were different from the church-going and camp-meeting type I'd ridden when I was younger. I could ride a horse fairly well as long as he went slow and straight, but if he turned quick, I fell off. Then Walter from across the herd would see me. He'd come loping around the back of the herd and help me up into the saddle again, then go on back to his side of the herd. Finally, after I kept falling off, he'd watch me for a while, and if I could get up and climb onto my horse, he figured I had no bones broken and must be okay, and he'd let me alone. When you fell off these horses, they stood and watched you get back on. They wouldn't run off.

After a few days, he put me on the older horses, more gentle. But still I fell off, especially if they speeded up a little. After he saw these horses were too quick, too, he got me an old plug. These were the kind of horses that were real old, worn out, and about all they could do was stump their toes on every rock or high place, and would stop every few minutes and grab a mouthful of grass. Now, since I was doing a little better, Walter thought he had fixed everything up. Not so much falling off. But the old horse and I would somehow get up too close to the front. Of course I was in the way. And pretty soon Walter would lose patience with me and call out, "Damn-it-to-*hell*, Sally [my pet name], get back behind."

Sometimes there would be fifteen or more cowboys along, professionals, and cowboys as good as there were anywhere along. But they never laughed at me. But sometimes, when I'd fallen off, I'd look at some of them nearby, and they were looking off. Neither did my father-in-law ever say anything. No advice, no caution, no nothing. They all let me alone. Guess they wanted me to learn cow punching the hard way. I always kept away from them and did my best not to be a bother. I always watched until they'd finished eating, get on their horses and leave, before I would go to the campfire and look for something to eat. I'd always find an iron skillet with meat, gravy, and beans, covered with fresh warm and soft cowboy bread. Then with the iron lid on top.

If we were going to some part of the big ranch where a wagon could not make it, then everything was packed on burros, the bedding and the camp outfit. If the chuck wagon could make it, everything was easier. All the equipment was easier to get to then. Water was tied in a keg on the outside of the wagon. The chuck box was set in the back end of the wagon. The door to it when it opened made a good table. Then the inside of the box made a nice kitchen cabinet, complete with shelves, places for tin plates, and dozens of cups. There were big iron kettles that I could hardly lift. Camp was complete when a big canvas fly was stretched across the top for shade.

I didn't know how to cook over a campfire or any other fire. Well, I just did not know much of anything. My father-in-law always had the men cook. He never corrected me or asked me to do anything. I guess he knew better. Neither did anyone else, including Walter. I could never tell when my father-in-law was laughing at me, he had so many whiskers and kept his hat pulled down over his eyes.

After a few weeks, when Walter thought I could ride better, he bought me a pretty little palomino mare. He says, "Now she's really gentle, and I think you can stay on her. Only thing, this man said she'd have to be watched, as she was very afraid of wasps and bees."

So he saddled her and I got up in the saddle and started out. I thought I was going to make it this time and began to be rather proud of myself and especially this pretty little animal. But we hadn't gone very far down the trail when here comes a big wasp flying by. My pretty mare made a big jump to one side, and I fell off. A hard fall this time. And as usual, Walter was close and saw it. The little palomino was sold, and I was back on the old plugs again.

After nearly two weeks of this outdoor living and trying to learn about horses and cows, I must have been very strong never to have broken a bone. In the mornings, I'd be a little sore. But I was always ready to try again. Only one time I ever heard one of the cowboys say a word was when I was getting back in the saddle after one of my falls. He said, "She's got what it takes." I thought that was silly. After all, getting back in the saddle again was about all you could do miles from anywhere. Riding and chancing a fall off was better than walking.

Sometimes we'd get so far from the main camp that we'd just stay all night where there was grass for the horses. We'd unsaddle, place the saddles on the ground, then take the saddle blankets which were wet with sweat and dust, put one on the ground to sleep on and use the other to cover with. The saddles at our heads kept the wind from blowing in our faces. All was fairly comfortable until the early morning hours. Then we'd nearly freeze sometimes.

My mother-in-law was a strong woman, too. She showed me how to run the traps at the ranch. The first time we went out, before we left the ranch, she says, "You'd better get the 410 shot gun. We'll need it to kill the varmints."

So I went back in the house and got the gun, come on out and climbed up on the horse with the gun, and lay it across the saddle in front of me. And we started out.

The first trap we came to had a big coyote. Right quick she says, "You're going to have to shoot him." I raised the gun to shoot, and it went off. And since my mother-in-law was in front of me, it just did miss her.

Not knowing what had happened, she said without looking around, "Did you hit him?" And she couldn't see I was shaking so bad I was speechless, and so scared I couldn't move. Neither had the horse moved. For one time, I was thankful for an old plug that was too old to untrack himself and didn't care whether you fell off or shot off him. Anyway, when I did get to the ground, the coyote was killed with rocks and sticks. I told her there were no more cartridges. I never did tell her the truth. Neither to this day have I told anyone. We kept on trapping the rest of the time, but without a gun. And the first dress I bought with my own money was after selling the hides.

One morning, one of the boys came in and said, "There's a big bunch of ducks swimming on the dirt tank." This was out close to the house.

My mother-in-law said, "Maybe you can take the shotgun and go kill a few."

I didn't think much of that idea, but I got the shotgun anyway. This time a twelve-gauge. I slipped out close to the tank, raised the gun, and sighted a duck. I thought sure I could kill a bunch this close, as the ducks were pretty close together. So when I thought I was ready, I pulled the trigger. Nothing happened. I studied a minute. Meanwhile, I lay the side of my face over the shotgun stock. I thought the gun was still sighted on the ducks. I pulled the trigger again. This time, the thing went off and so did part of my face. It felt like it anyway. The ducks all flew off unharmed. So there were more excuses to be made as to why I didn't bring home the ducks.

My mother-in-law always give me big things to do. Seems she thought I could do anything. And when I failed, which I always did, she never said a thing. Just thought of something else. Whatever it was, I never said no. I always remember seven great people in my life: my mother, Norah Bosworth, and my daddy, Luke Wilson. My grandparents, Doc and Lucindy Belle Starr Wilson. My father- and mother-in-law, William Isaac "Bill Ike" Babb and Laura Alice Lewis Babb. And my husband, Walter Babb. My mother-in-law was the one that learned me how to work, especially outside.

She taught me a lot, too, about using the plants in that part of the country. We made jelly in the season. Used the tunas off the prickly pear. Pear apples. When the pear apples get ripe, you don't take the thorns off of them, just see that they're clean, wash them off. Then you put them in a great big pot and cover them with water. Set them on to boil. Then take a big masher of some kind and mash all these tunas up for sauce. And when the water is red, you don't cook it any longer because if you cook it, the color will start to leave. So while it's red, you pour this whole thing through a straining cloth. You strain all of the sediment out, the seeds and the skins, strain all that out, and that leaves you with just the juice. And with that juice, you make jelly just like you do with anything else.

Aguavilla[2] berries, too. It's a bush that looks like a holly berry. Grows red berries all over the whole bush. So we used to wait til it got ripe. Then we put this sheet all around this bush, then took a stick and beat the berries off, and they all fell in this sheet. We'd put the berries in a box or bucket, and there'd be all kinds of trash with it from beating them. So you couldn't pick it all out. So we'd take a wet tow sack and put one end in a tub. Somebody would hold it back at the end, and we'd pour the little berries in the top of that, and the berries would roll down, but the fibers of the sack would trap the trash. So that was the way we could clean them. And we done them the same way as prickly pear. We cooked them, strained them, and used the juice. And that was good, too. So that was our jelly. And their flowers have a smell that nothing else does. A good sweet smell.

The first winter, my mother-in-law gave Walter and me a feather mattress. Then a friend of Walter's told him he had a small tent we could have. So we were real tickled. A tent and a feather mattress. First time we went to line camp way off in the mountains, Walter packed everything on a burro. And by this time I could ride a little better, but was still on an old horse.

When evening came, we stopped, and Walter and Bill set up camp. They stretched the tent as well as they knew how. Then they put the feather mattress in the tent on the ground. Everything looked so nice until we got into bed. Then when we stretched out, the tent was too short, and our feet would reach outside in the cold.

Soon, not only could I ride better, I could cook a few things on the campfire. But I reckon Walter still didn't trust me to cook for him as he got three frying pans, one for him, one for me, and the other for Bill. He'd get out the sack of jerky, give me a knife, and tell me to cut up what meat I could eat. Then he'd do the same, and on to Bill. Then each of us would cover the dried meat with water and put our frying pans on the hot coals to boil until the meat was tender. Then potatoes, garlic, onions, tomatoes, and a little flour was added. About this time, Walter would tell Bill to go get a bucket of water. Since the water was a good ways off, Walter would be safe in stealing some of Bill's stew. When Bill came back and the stew was ready to eat, he'd always finish his meal first. Then he'd look all around and say, "Dad burn it, I'm still hungry."

Walter would be very generous and give him some of his stew. We each ate out of the frying pans. We had no plates. Our bread was always a little short and on these trips got old, hard, and dry. Mostly it was loaves of cowboy bread tied up in flour sacks. You make it the same as biscuit dough, except you don't put grease in it. You kind of fry it in grease. Have the skillet hot and greased. Flatten it out so that it'll cook through, and when it's brown on one side, flip it over and brown the other. That's what the men would cook on the campfire.

Sometimes a goat- or sheepherder let us have beans to eat. The beans were real soft and good. The herders would take a molasses bucket with a lid that could be put on real tight, punch two or three holes in the lid, and fill it about one-fourth full of beans, then finish filling it with water, salt, and bacon or salt pork. Then the bucket was placed in the middle of hot ashes and coals, the ashes were raked up all around the bucket of beans clear to the top, then left, no fire at all. By two o'clock the beans were soft.

When shearing time came, there were sometimes as many as two thousand or more Angora goats to shear, and no more than eight or ten men to shear the goats. Everybody was very busy and hurrying around. My mother-in-law told me I could help by going to the pens and tying up the corners of the wool sacks. I knew the corners of each sack of wool had a sort of knot where the men could handle them better, and it had always looked to me like it might have rocks tied in each corner. So I got busy and gathered some rocks and tied them real good in each corner of the wool sacks. Then when I'd finished, I went back to the house. She said, "Did you get the sacks ready?"

I said, "Oh, yes."

She said, "What did you put in the corners?"

I said, "Rocks."

Well, that was one time she nearly fell over. Then she said, "Don't you know? The corners are made from little balls of wool or mohair."

Then after shearing, most of the time the sheep and goats were dipped to kill the lice that were on them. There was a big cement vat, and it was filled with warm sulphur water. The vat was pretty long, and at each end there were pens, one to hold the sheep or goats to be pushed off in the water. The other had a slanting cement slab where the animals could swim on out and stand a while so that the water would drip off them and run back into the vat.

As the goats or sheep were pushed off into the sulphur water, men with forked sticks would push their heads completely under the water and keep this up until they swam out and stood on the cement to drain. When all the men got on either side with their long poles, I asked for a pole, too. One was handed to me. So I went to the middle of the vat. The sulphur water was deeper there. I was trying to push the animals' heads down under the water, when my foot slipped, and in another second I'd have been in the strong sulphur water with the goats and sheep. But at once a hand grabbed my arm and I was pulled back. It was Walter. When I was far enough away from the vat, he turned my arm loose and said, "Sally, you'd better go back to the house and help ma wash dishes." When the goat and sheep dipping was over, all the men left. My mother-in-law and I was alone again.

One day she said, "In the morning, we'll saddle our horses and go bring in a real fat yearling calf. We'll kill it and have some fresh meat."

As she kept on talking, I could just taste a juicy roast—the kind she made. So next morning after our work was done, we got the two horses that were in the pen, brought them out, and put the saddles on. They seemed real gentle. When we were ready, we started out to a certain pasture five or six miles away. We went through the gate and then rode on quite a ways before we found any cattle. Meanwhile, my horse acted like he was asleep and had to be prodded along with a quirt. We finally found several head of cattle grazing along. My mother-in-law said, "There's a dandy. Let's cut him out."

By this time, the cattle had started running, so I gave the horse a rather hard lick with the quirt. He woke up and started after the cattle. There was a big bush in the way. I was thinking the horse and I would go to the right of it, when he dodged and went to the left. I fell off right in the middle of this thorny bush and was just stuck there in the thorns. I don't know what kind of bush it was, as I didn't know one plant from another at the time.

My horse stopped, and I could see my mother-in-law coming, but she wasn't coming very fast. I was full of thorns and blood was all over my face, my hands, arms, and legs, and blood was coming through my clothes here and there all over my body. She finally got to me and pulled me out of the thorns. She picked all the thorns she could out of me. Then she brushed me off a little. Neither of us were talking. Finally, after she'd got a lot of the thorns out, as many as she could find, she helped me back on my horse. Then she said, "We'll leave the cattle alone for this time."

When we finally got to the ranch and I washed up, I was not hurt so bad after all.

Some of the ranchers began to buy Model T Fords. So my mother-in-law decided she'd buy one just for herself, as she was milking lots of cows, and the hens were laying good. She'd get dozens of eggs a day, and, by having a car, she could drive twenty-six miles to town and sell the milk and eggs and butter. She was raising a grandson at the time, my brother-in-law's boy, and one day a man asked him how many cows they milked. He said, "Seventeen."

Then the man says, "How much milk do you get a day?"

The grandson says, "Seventeen pints."

Anyway, she got the car and learned how to drive it. She would save up all the milk, butter, and eggs for a week. We had no ice box, but a kind of water cooler. Then on a certain day, milk, butter, and eggs were packed in the new car and she would drive the twenty-six miles to the nearest little town to peddle it out. She'd sell most all the eggs, milk, and butter before starting back home, twenty-six miles again on a rough dirt road. She never stopped or slowed down for a ditch in the road. And a curve, if it was possible, she would cut straight through instead of following the road. We would always try to get back to the ranch early. So this time, we got back to the ranch the middle of the evening. And instead of going around to the back of the house, as she usually did, she headed straight for the front and the paling fence where all her chickens, turkeys, ducks, and geese were gathered in the shade of the fence. I kept thinking we would stop. But no, the brakes had quit working. And the car went right into the fence, then right on top and stopped. Chickens and all underneath the fence and car. Killed most of the chickens and a lot was crippled.

It was time to check the line camps. So this time, Walter said I could go with them. The burro was packed and we started out. Takened half a day to get to the camp in the canyons. We got there at night. The next morning Walter said, "I got to go kill a deer." They were very plentiful. So he saddled my horse and we didn't go very far when we saw several big bucks close by. He shot at the nearest buck and it fell. He says, "Run, Sally, and set on his neck and hold his horn. Try to keep him down while I kill the other one."

I went and sat on the deer's neck and held onto his horns. And it did not try to get up, just lay there quiet. Walter killed the other deer and hurried on back to me and says, "Now you can get up off his neck, and I'll finish killing him."

I got up and so did the deer, running off as fast as he could. He didn't seem to be hurt at all, and Walter's gun was too far away for him to get it.

Soon, Walter and my mother-in-law began learning me how to drive the Model T. And I seemed to be better at driving a car than riding horses. And I thought I learned pretty fast. One evening we'd gone somewhere, and as we came back to the ranch and stopped a ways from the old plank barn, they all went into the house, and I thought to myself that I would put the car in the barn. I started the motor and got in. Everything worked fine, and I headed it into the barn. But instead of going straight through the door, I went through the side.

I always washed a lot of dishes for my mother-in-law. If I went off for a week and come back, I washed what dirty dishes there was. And she began learning me to cook a few things. And soon it was springtime. She had around two hundred head of Angora nannies to kid. When kids began to come, it was an all-day job and part of most of the night. All the kids were staked by one foot on a little rope with swivels in front of a tiny steel box with an opening in front for the kids to get in out of the sun or rain. The rope would have to be changed each day to keep the kid from hurting itself or causing its legs to swell. And after a day or so, each nannie would know exactly where her kid was and go and suckle it. Some of the old nannies would seem to want to forget where their kids were. They had to be caught and dragged clear across the pen and held to let their babies nurse.

I was good at working with the goats, and we had no trouble. Most of the time just the two of us were there, as the men were off working on different parts of the ranch and did not come back very often. When the kids were up bigger and most had been turned loose with their mommas, then we had to wash six weeks of clothes if the men were around, but they would help, too. They'd put the big iron pots on the rocks, fill them up with water carried from the tank, and build a big fire around the pots. Big chunks of homemade lye soap was chipped up in the pots of water when it boiled, and all the soap was melted. It made pretty soap suds. All the clothes had to be washed on a board first. Then when the clothes were clean, they were dropped in the big iron pots to boil a while in these strong soap suds. Then they were finally takened out of hot suds in the pots and washed again, and, this time, they were rung out and ready to rinse in two big tubs of clear water. They were wrung out the last time and hung on the line. When there was no more lines, then we spread them on trees, fences, or whatever would hold them up to dry. All the time when the clothes were drying, the cows had to be watched and run off, as they'd chew a lot of the clothes up. Work clothes were not ironed. There were too many of them. We just ironed the nice shirts and pants. And when it was possible, the ironing was takened to Mexican women in town to iron.

Walter and I had gone to a little house at one of the line camps. The house wasn't so bad. It had a cookstove and table and chairs and a bed in it. One morning, Walter and Bill rode off to count goats and sheep. While they were gone, I thought how nice it would be if I'd make them a ginger cake. I had all the things to make it with, spices and all that. But I'd only seen Mrs. Babb or my mother make up the dough, and didn't see the measures. So I thought, well, surely that will be easy. I won't need to measure anything. So I put what I thought it would take of this and that. And stirred it all up. Put flour and molasses and sugar. Milk. When I thought it was ready to bake, I put it in the pan. Then in the oven. After a while when it had time to be ready, I looked at the cake in the oven, and it was just a liquid. All molasses. I thought that I'd better not let the men see this. So I takened it out of the stove, went behind the house, and poured it out. Of course the dogs ate it soon as it was cool enough. So I thought the men would never have to know. That evening, when Walter and Bill walked into the house, the first thing Walter says is, "What's that I smell?" But the molasses ginger cake I had poured outside and the hound dogs ate it before Walter and Bill got home.

All through these months of mistakes one right after the other, the whole family were very patient with me, and I never got a scolding. I still look back and don't understand it. These were strong, hardy men, hard workers ready to fight at the drop of a hat. They were called dangerous men. Yet, they all put up with me. When any of the family quarreled, I figured it was none of my business, as I knew they'd quarreled and fought all their lives. And who was I to get into their affairs?

One time two of the brothers got into a big fight. Just the two of them. Four or five miles away from the ranch. They come in, finally, on their horses, all cut up and bleeding. They'd used their knives on each other.

Another time, I went with Walter and Mr. Babb on a roundup. About seven miles from headquarters along with some cowboys and hired hands. After being there nearly a week, Mr. Babb was out of tobacco. And all the men were busy, so they asked me if I thought I could go to headquarters in a buggy or hack. When I was a child riding here and there in the wagon, my daddy and grandpa had let me ride up on the front seat with them sometimes, and sometimes let me hold the reins and drive. So I'd learned a little on how to hold the reins and drive two horses. So I told Walter I believed I could make it to the ranch after the tobacco.

They hitched up two nice fat horses, and as I climbed up in the seat, Mr. Babb said, "Now don't go too fast. Try to keep the horses at a slow trot."

Well, I started out not too fast. Finally, after I'd gone three or four miles, I thought the horses could go a bit faster. So I hit them a few times with the reins, and they nearly ran away. A big log was on one side of the road. The buggy run over it, nearly turning over. And I nearly fell out. After the horses had settled down, I didn't try to go fast anymore. I got to the ranch at sundown, stayed all night, and the next morning early I started back with the tobacco. And I didn't have any more trouble.

Along about this time, I knew I was to have my first baby in seven or eight months. So I had to quit all the horseback riding and such things. My sister-in-law ordered me medicine from New York to take the entire time I was carrying the baby so that I would keep strong and so the baby would also be strong and healthy and have good strong teeth and bones. Mrs. Babb did not care how much you worked when you wasn't pregnant. But she sure watched out for her daughters-in-law before they were to have babies. She would see to it that they moved to town to be near a doctor, although she was a wonderful midwife herself, as well as knowing how to care for the sick.

So I went into town to be with my parents. My grandma said never lift anything heavy. And never bend down, like under a fence, because the cord would wrap around the baby's neck. So you weren't supposed to bend down, and you weren't supposed to reach up too high. You were never to look at anything that looked ugly, or if a child or anyone come in with blood on them, you shouldn't look at that because, when the baby came, it'd have blood there, too. A bloodmark. My sister-in-law had one on her baby. On its face. She knew when she saw it what had happened. One of the children had fallen down and there was a whole lot of blood on his face, and she just put her hand up like that. So when the baby came, there was the red mark.[3]

I'd call the doctor when it was time. Then afterwards I'd stay in bed twelve days. My grandmother knew a lot, and she said you have to stay in bed twelve days. And I did. And that's the way to be healthy. Well, my heavens, anyone who's got any sense at all knows that getting up so quick is no good. So I'd lay in bed twelve days. I wouldn't even raise up. You wouldn't hardly raise up in those days. You just stayed on your back. Most every woman in those days did that.

Finally, the time came when Walter Dillard Babb arrived. I certainly did not know what to do with a tiny baby. So my own momma made me stay with her for six weeks so that she could learn me how to take care of him. Finally, Walter came and got me, and we went back to the ranch. I was lucky, as we stayed with Mrs. Babb. Since she'd raised ten children, she knew what to do and helped me.

Of course I breast-fed. And then, in maybe about six weeks, I would start him on a little milk gravy. Gravy was the main thing, and then later what we'd eat, if it was soft. Beans we mashed up, and soup, tomato gravy, soft crumbs of bread. I was raised on dime brand—Eagle Brand. My momma always says, "She can't have but a little, what it says on the can." Meantime, I was hollering and crying, and my grandparents would give me the whole can. So I'd eat all I wanted. And Dixie was about the same way.

Then, after a few more months, we moved to an isolated ranch, and I was alone as to help with Dixie, which is what we called the new baby. One day Walter wanted to go somewhere, and I started to dress Dixie. He had little white shoes, and they were dirty. I thought I could wash them right quick, then put them in the oven to dry. Well, I did. After a few minutes, I opened the stove door to get his shoes and they'd just dried up. They were about two inches long.

After he was able to set up, I'd put him on a pillow in front of me. I'd get up on the horse. Then Walter would hand me a pillow, and I'd place it in front of me. Then Dixie, he would set next to me in front. So we would start out. Sometimes we had to go six or seven miles. If he got sleepy, he just stretched out, and I held him on the pillow.

One time we had to go to another ranch across the Pecos River. A ranch hand went with us. When we got to the Pecos River, to me it looked half a mile wide. Big logs floating down in the dark muddy waters. I didn't know whether to be scared or not, but it sure didn't look possible to me on horseback. But when we got to the edge, Walter takened the baby Dixie in front of him. Bill and him got below me. Reckon they thought I'd get scared and fall off, and if they were where they could pull me out of the water, I'd be safer. Walter says, "Now don't look at the water. Just look at the land over on the other side."

We started. Water got deeper and swifter, and as we got near the middle, the waters came up above the horse's side and nearly into the saddle. Maybe the horses were swimming. I didn't know. Anyway, after a long time, seemed to me, the horses were wading out on the other side. Only then did it seem my heart started beating again. We went on to the other ranch and stayed a few days. When we started back and came to the Pecos River, it was down and had just a little water in it. So we crossed this time in a few minutes without trouble.

Each time we had to go somewhere, Dixie rode in front of me. This kept up until the second baby, Wilson Irvin, came. Then Dixie had to be tied on a burro. Sometimes, when it was cold, a blanket or quilt was wrapped around him, tied and pinned so that it would not come off. And since the animal was a pack burro, he knew how to follow us and stay close behind.

I had set some traps out, so one morning I had to go to see about them. I could leave Dixie with some men. But Irvin I had to put on the horse in front of me and take him along. We passed several traps before we came to one with a fox. I got down off the horse, and since Irvin could set up pretty good, I thought he would be all right setting on the horse while I killed the fox. So I left him on the horse. In a few minutes, I heard something hit the ground. I looked up, and it was Irvin on the ground. I was sure scared. But he didn't cry very much and seemed okay. The horse hadn't moved. I picked Irvin up and set him on the ground where I thought he'd be safe. Then I finished killing the fox and tied it on the back of my saddle. After looking at my other traps, we went on home.

A few weeks after this, Walter had to go to another ranch again. Dixie was tied on the pack burro. Irvin was on the pillow in front of me. And we started out. Everything was doing fine until we came to a very steep mountain. Walter was in the lead. He came to a steep part of the trail and started down, and I followed him. We came to about the steepest place in the trail, and my saddle started slipping over the horse's head. In a few seconds, the horse lowered his head. And Irvin on his pillow and me right behind went off over the horse's head and fell on this steep place. Somehow Irvin fell on the pillow and me on top of him. It didn't even scare Irvin. Walter got off his horse, walked back up the trail, saddled the horse again, and I got back in the saddle with Irvin and his pillow. Neither of us were hurt.

Sometimes we would camp along the banks of the Pecos. There were crevices in the rocks underneath the water where sixty-five–to–seventy–pound catfish would be in the holes. Walter would spear them. Sometimes he'd take a butcher knife and tie it on a stick to make the spear. He'd take their entrails out and hang them in the kitchen. You sure don't want any fish after that. He'd give them to the neighbors, but I haven't liked fish since then.

Mr. Babb had so many sections down there around Langtry that they had one ranch, one big ranch, over here, then another one over here, just all these ranches and cattle, horses, bulls, goats, and sheep. Sometimes twenty-five hundred Angoras. All over this whole country they owned, with a herder or a caretaker with these goats. Then they had to have a line rider that goes from one place to another on horseback for relief for the herders. When you have a bunch of stock here and another over here and another over here, each with a man taking care of them, then you have to have an overseer, and that was called the line rider. So that is what Walter was. And sometimes I would go with him, even after the first two children were born. Sometimes we takened a chuck wagon, and sometimes we didn't have no chuck wagon. And when we got on up there, we would have a tent and I would cook a meal. And we had seventeen hounds one time. So they was into everything just like these dogs here, into everything on the place. And even if you fed them the best meat, they still stole everything they could get ahold of. So I'd cook and put everything on the table. We had boards up for a table top, put across something, and I'd cook and put everything on this table. And step outside and—didn't have a door, see, tents—step outside and call the men to dinner. And when I come back, the dogs had just cleaned everything off the table.

And the cowboys, they always would get around the campfire to eat breakfast. And they'd all walk to the pen and rope their horse and bring the horse up close to the fire. They'd saddle the horses, and there'd be around seven or eight, maybe more. They'd saddle the horses, and one of them would go pitching and would go right into the fire, across everything, just scatter pots and pans and beans and coffee, and then sometimes one of the men would get out and throw his hat under the horses to make them pitch. So there the horse was, going this way and that, and maybe a man would fall and maybe he wouldn't.

In camp the two children, Irvin and Dixie, would go in the wagon or on horseback. If there wasn't any chuck wagon, they used pack mules or burros. We'd spread a big tarp or canvas around out in the open, put what quilts we had down, then pull the tarp up over the bed and over our heads. The two babies slept with us. And then along toward daylight, when it got cold, the dogs would all get down around us, and that kept us warm. I hate dogs—I've hated them always. But I didn't hate them then. We always had hounds. You have to have them for the varmints. I think a white shepherd has more sense than anything, but they kill so.

When we did get up in the mornings, snow sometimes covered the canvas that was on top of our bed. The children would be wrapped up in a quilt, and I carried them to the big campfire to dress them. That would be after all the cowboys were gone. They would always leave something cooked in the big iron skillets—deer meat and gravy, cowboy bread, mashed beans with salt pork fried, and strong coffee. That cowboy life. For women. You can learn a lot. I think it's good for you if you can do it. The only thing that'll hurt a person is, like I say, stress. And that'll kill your body. But work won't. But that kind of life makes you depend on yourself when it comes to sickness. I learned a lot about that. I took care of my children and animals both.

Like one time, Irvin, the middle boy, had played in the mud. So he had gone in the house and taken a hot bath. And then he got in the truck in the back of it. So that night a cold norther come, and when he went to bed he was all tight—oh, he was tight. Pneumonia, you see, or something like. Anyhow, I had the Musterol.[4] So I takened the Musterol, some turpentine, and a little coal oil and rubbed it all over his chest. So finally he went to sleep, and the next morning he had blisters all over his chest, but he didn't have any more cold. It must've just brought it all out.

So that's when I first started, I guess. Well, you had to be a doctor and you had to be a nurse if you was going to take care of a young baby 100, 150 miles from a town. All four of them was healthy. The last one, a girl. Wayne was born in 1925, then Azalea come along. By that time I was staying pretty close to the ranch. We had a ranch of our own, and I wasn't getting out as much, but always helped with the goats and sheep.

And I learned to take care of the animals, too. I remember the goats would get sore mouth,[5] and they'd get worms in their mouth. It was terrible. So the first time that the sore mouth vaccine come out, we vaccinated babies. Goats and lambs. So the first time we used it, I was out in the pen helping them like all women do down there in that country. So I was vaccinating them right under their hind legs. And so I taken the sore mouth, and I guess I gave it to the children, too. I guess I wasn't washing off then. I didn't know—I wasn't too smart. But anyhow, the whole family taken the sore mouth—sores around the mouth. The animals will have the sores, and they'll bleed, and then the flies will lay eggs there, you see. We didn't do that, but we did have the sores for about ten days. Not much you can do for it. Nothing tastes good. So we've always laughed about that. And one time at the ranch here, I had goats and they taken sore mouth. So one little nanny had her mouth just swelled out awful, with big scabs on it. So she was in the habit of coming and raring up on my back and putting her feet up on me, you know. And somebody said, "Oh, you're going to take sore mouth." And I said, "No, I done had it." When you have it one time, you don't have it any more.

All the women worked, all in that country. And at kidding time, at lambing time, the little lambs were brought in around the stove, and we put down tow sacks to save them. We wouldn't leave them outside. Not all of them, but the weaker ones, sometimes fifteen or so in the house until the cold spell was over. One time I raised ninety-two lambs and kids. That must have been about 1923, back there. We didn't think too much about the housekeeping. I knew that if we raised them, there'd be that much more money.

But there was only one time any of my children really got sick. But I took care of him then. That was little Irvin again. He got sick with diarrhea, and we got bark and made tea. You can use mesquite bark or oak bark, boil it and make tea out of it.[6] Don't make it too strong. That helped him, but he sure liked to died. There weren't anyone around to help me at the time. Just hired hands. Just men. Mexican hired hands.

And we learned how to depend on ourselves in other ways, too. Financial ways. Like during the Depression. I always liked milk cows. So one evening Walter came in, and he was mad. He said, "You know what? One of our friends wanted to sell me some old poor Jersey cows." And he said, "I don't want no Jersey cows!" Ranchers don't like Jersey cows. He said, "I told him I wouldn't want Jersey cows—just six of them for $150.00."

I said, "Well, you go right over and tell him we'll take those cows." And then he really got mad. He said, "We don't want them cows."

I said, "Get them, because there's money in them."

Well, I wore him down. So he went to the phone and told that man we'd take the cows. So a few days later, here come George out at the ranch with the scrawniest looking Jersey cows you ever seen. They didn't hardly look worth anything. Only one of them was giving milk. So we fed her up and milked her because she was giving milk. Then a month or so later, we went into Langtry and rented this little house because it was time for the kids to go to school. And so every time I milked this cow, there was an old woman who come to the back door holding this little pan out, and she says, "I want a dime's worth milk." Every morning, every time I milked, she wanted a dime's worth. So most every time I'd give her about this much milk, and she'd give a dime. Milk was selling for a dime a quart in those days. So that was about all the milk I was selling about then.

Anyhow, we had bought a new bobtailed truck, a big one, and we didn't pay any money because all you had to do was give a check. Everything was easy. But we got up the next morning, and everything was closed. We couldn't get no money nowhere. So I told my husband, "You go to the ranch." It must've been about twelve months since we first got the cows, and by that time they were in better shape, and one or two of them had calves. And I said, "You bring me another cow, and I'll sell milk. I'll milk them and sell milk." Well, I did. And it kept on. We couldn't get no money nowhere. Things had all closed. And Walter didn't have a salary, being a rancher, so he brought another cow in. And by that time, I was milking two cows, selling milk a dime a quart. And the little boys, Irvin and Dixie, would deliver. They'd walk on down the street carrying it to the houses, and they'd always make it pretty good unless they stopped and shot marbles in the middle of the street or have a fight. But finally they'd get there.

So about that time, a big construction outfit came into Langtry, and they began to need milk. I said, "Bring some more cows." Kept on til I was milking seven twice a day. So I don't know how much I was getting, but maybe I was making three or four dollars a day at the time, because they was better milk cows than we thought they was. And the boys delivering it and helping me. And Mr. Babb had a farm with lots of cane hay, so we hauled this hay in for the cows. And Walter went out on the weekend and chopped wood and sold it to the people. Put it in the big truck that we were making big payments on and hauled wood on the weekend to the construction people, and that was pretty good money. Then a lot of times at night, he'd go down to these people, and he'd shoot dice with them, and he won all the time! Wood and that and milk, and we'd save up enough every month to make payments on that truck. Payments were a hundred dollars probably. A family right close to us said, "Well, I think she's crazy milking them ol' cows." And they had bought a big fine car, and they lost it. But we didn't lose the truck. So that went on six months. And I'd make pies for the restaurant sometimes, too. And sometimes I'd iron, get a little money that way. The construction workers, you see, they'd get paid pretty good. And when the banks opened, we didn't go and ask for money. Because we was making a little. And the banker saw my husband and said, "We want to know what you're doing, because everybody else has come and asked for money, but you haven't."

I don't know how long the banks was closed, because I was young and didn't keep track of things. Must have been six or seven months. But we made it.

CHAPTER 5

The Trappers

I SPENT my second stay with Mrs. Babb alone, as Chuck remained in El Paso to take care of Brookie and to return to his classes. Mrs. Babb had a houseful throughout the period of time I was with her, as Wayne Babb and his trapping crew were in and out every day. This was the first opportunity I had to talk with Wayne Babb, and I found that his stories provided further insights into Mrs. Babb's own life-style.

The first morning, Mrs. Babb cooked a huge breakfast: scrambled eggs, bacon, fried potatoes. She told me to put out a new jar of apple preserves and whatever else I could find. She had a refrigerator, but it really didn't keep anything cool. She used the shelves for storage more than anything else. There was a table underneath the back window in the kitchen where perishables were piled. We put the fruit and vegetables in tins at night to keep from attracting mice. I took bread and margarine from the refrigerator and apples, oranges, and peanut butter from the table and put them out for breakfast, too. The stove was very old and crusted over on the top so that all the pans and skillets were smoked up and black. Mrs. Babb was impatient with it while she cooked. "This ol' stove burns up everything," she said, and "whew! whew!" "Whew" is one of her favorite words. It takes the place of a curse. She generally makes a fanning gesture with her hand when she uses it—directed toward the stove, her grandchildren when they are rowdy, the old goat trying to get in the back door.

Wayne Babb was still asleep in one of the small bedrooms off the dining room. His helper, J. W. Young, was asleep on a pile of bedding on the dining room floor, and in the living room was a pallet with two of Wayne's children who had been out trapping with him: Richard and Nute. They were just beginning to stir as we put breakfast on the table. Despite the lack of conveniences, I liked working in Mrs. Babb's kitchen. There was always a show to be seen through the long, low window that looked out onto the goat pen in the backyard. The goats' playfulness with each other, their little squabbles, and their making-up gestures were a pleasure to watch. That morning there was a new arrival on the scene, which Mrs. Babb pointed out to me, and we stopped the breakfast preparations long enough to do some observing. Behind the white rooster was a small red hen. She pecked on the ground behind him, apparently unaware that he was there, yet never more than three or four steps away from him. He was walking his usual guard around the goat pen with her behind him. Mrs. Babb said the chicken was probably from the house on the other side of the road. I could see why the hen had lost her heart to the white rooster. He certainly had quite a flair, and his neck seemed to arch even more with the red hen behind him, although he gave her no overt attention.

After watching the chickens for a while, I finished setting the table, then stuck my head into Wayne's bedroom and called him for breakfast. Soon the trapping crew gathered around the table, jostling each other for the scrambled eggs. Everyone drank coffee. Nute, the younger of the two boys, drank his with lots of milk and sugar. He was talkative that morning, as usual, and was telling us the story of how he had put rabbits in a tow sack the night before. He used his fork to gesture and illustrate the story. Richard, who was sixteen, was a quiet boy and didn't talk much at all. J. W. was from Arkansas. He was in his early twenties and had shaggy, long blond hair and a full blond beard with a reddish cast to it. When I asked him how he came to be in Valentine, he said he was hitchhiking through, not going much of anywhere, when he met Wayne. He had been working for Wayne for the past two months.

Wayne was a tall, spare man, his face tanned like hide from so many years spent outside. He was fifty-three years old but had the wiriness and strength of body of a much younger man. His hair showed only a little gray, and his face had only the sharp creases from nose to mouth that so many ranchers seem to develop from grimacing into the sun. He had worked on and off as a trapper all his life. When he was a boy, he trapped ringtails for five or six dollars apiece, he told me. "I'd catch 'em while I was growing up. Always have money in my pockets."[1] Twice he trapped for the government. "You go to different ranches where they need you and you have to make different reports. They pay salary and mileage. I worked back in the forties that way, but they didn't pay so much. You had to cut the ears off. Tell how many you caught and where you caught 'em." He was talking about panthers, bobcats, and coyotes primarily, the pests which the ranchers in this part of the country hate. He said a panther can travel twenty-five to thirty miles a day and can kill a hundred sheep in a night. He said that when he was younger he could see ten or twelve deer during a day of just riding around—bucks, does, and fawns. But now the numbers have been decimated. The rivers have been fished out, and the hunting isn't as good. These conditions have made panthers more of a problem, as the cattle and goat herds are their only source of meat.

For the past several years, though, Wayne has trapped independently. He had approximately fifty traps out and tried to run them once a day. They covered ten square miles, and he was working an area some fifteen miles south of Van Horn. He had gotten permission from the ranchers to trap on their land, and he was using number-three and number-four traps, catching bobcats, coyotes, foxes, ringtails, and badgers. He also trapped from time to time in the lower country around Ozona and Uvalde, catching skunks, ringtails, racoons, badgers, bobcats, and possums. He could get $60.00 to $65.00 apiece, $70.00 for an especially good hide. Twenty-four lynx cat hides, he said, go to make a woman's coat, and the final selling price might be close to $8,000.00.

In addition to trapping, Wayne and J. W. pulled out various cacti in the desert and sold them to nurserymen in El Paso and, occasionally, in New Mexico and Arizona.

"We ask 'em, you want the hippies?" Wayne and J. W. laughed over that. The hippies are what they call the tall yuccas when the dead leaves up and down the stalk have not been trimmed, as the yucca has a distinctly human look, its long stalk tending to bend gracefully at what would be the waist and the sudden bush of leaves looking like untidy hair at the top.

J. W. giggled at the joke. "Yep, they sure love them hippies all right." J. W. pulled something out of his pocket to show me. It was a button cactus, which they had been gathering the day before. It was a tight little ball of soft white spines in small star clusters. J. W. said they grow in clusters together, soft like toes.

This precipitated a discussion of useful plants in the area. Wayne Babb contributed as much as his mother to the conversation. J. W. was comparatively new to the region but expressed a high degree of interest in plant information.

"Star cactus[2] is a good cure for rheumatism. You cut it up, boil it, and drink it," Mrs. Babb told me. This, apparently, was the local name for the cactus I was holding in my hand.

"Evan Means cuts it up and puts it in his whiskey," Wayne said.

"Who's Evan Means?" I asked him.

"Oh, he's about ninety-six years old, little bitty ol' guy with a big black mustache, looks like a Mexican. Cooks on a wood stove like a hundred years ago. Lives in an old hut, you know. He weighs about seventy-five pounds, little ol' tiny guy, big mustache. He don't allow a radio on the place, no electricity; when it's dark, he goes to bed, then gets up early. He's got a big tree, and a spring of water comes up around the house, and he'll get up there and get him a bucket of water. And he don't have to pay no water bills. Has a kerosene lantern. Evan Means."

"Sounds like he and your mother have a lot in common," I said. Wayne laughed, but Mrs. Babb, suppressing a smile, returned to the original discussion.

"Star cactus is good for constipation, too," she said. "And for rheumatism, the prickly pear is good. You use the big, light green one.[3] Then there's one good root in this country that I like. It's called bloodroot, and when you dig it up, it starts bleeding, just like blood, and that's good for pyorrhea of the teeth. And for your stomach. And then you go down deeper til the root just thins off like that. And if you're out in the pasture and you get thirsty and don't have no water, you can dig up one of those roots and just eat it, you know, and it's just full of water. Bloodroot or *sanguinaria*. Lots of people say there's no such name. But that's what they call it, the Mexicans: *sanguinaria*.[4]

"And then there's a plant in this country, used to grow down in our country but was smaller down there, and we'd dig it up, and the root makes soap. It's soapy. But here it grows bigger, and it's called Joshuay Tree. We could use our kind for soap, to wash your hair with and everything. Just take a piece and put it in the water."[5]

"When do things start blooming around here?" I asked.

"March and April," Mrs. Babb replied. "The yuccas start blooming the seventeenth of March. They say you can boil the flowers up, just like cabbage. But I've eaten them raw. They're good and sweet tasting, kind of like lettuce. And the goats, oh, my! They come in March, these flowers do, and the goats are so glad to get them, they just eat them up like that.

"But my favorite plant is *Aloe vera*. I always say that there's three things I can grow real good, and that's goats, white shepherds, and *Aloe vera.* That *Aloe vera* is what I put on my burn the other day. Wayne said it was a second- or third-degree burn, and it's just fine now." She looked up at Wayne, who nodded in confirmation. "It's good for your eyes, too. Put it in your eyes, rub it like this. Open the leaf up, and be sure the thorn's gone. I used it yesterday and the day before for mine, because I guess I'm allergic to this alfalfa. And ever time I use that hay, my eyes get red."

"And then there's tequila," Wayne said. He and J. W. laughed at the switch from *Aloe vera* to strong drink. "Take heads of sotol and cook them up. Vats of sotol heads.[6] Let it soak. Then mash it up with your feet. At least that's the way they do it in Mexico.

"And then, you ever heard of candelilla? We all used to make money on that out there at the hot springs. You get a big vat about eight feet long, and about three and a half feet deep. Then haul the weed in on a donkey stacked up. Get sulphuric acid. Then you make a fire using wood. After you get started cooking weed in the water, add two cups of sulphuric acid. The acid cuts the wax away from the weed, and it comes to the top. Then dip the wax into a barrel. Then fish out the weed, dry it out, and use for wood the next time instead of wood. About forty to forty-five pounds of weed will make one pound of wax. Johnson's Floor Wax used it. A weigher would weigh it when the Mexicans brought it in on burros. And when it was hot and dry, the weed had more wax."[7]

After breakfast, Nute took me around the side of the house. There was a dead bobcat lying along the path to the backyard. Stretched out like that, it was about four feet long. The coat was a soft light brown. It looked very much like one of my housecats back in El Paso on a slightly larger scale. Nute hopped on top of it, jumping up and down. He stuck a finger in its mouth and tried to pull up the stiffened lip to expose the teeth. He wanted me to take a photograph of him on top of the cat, but I told him I was out of film.

It was a day of routine chores. I did not follow the activities in the yard, although I knew well enough that the bobcat would be skinned and the carcass given to the dogs to eat. Instead, I washed dishes, then cleaned up the living room, folding up the pallet the two boys had slept on the night before. Mrs. Babb spent the day writing, and I worked on my notes. Wayne and J. W. spent much of the day trying to get their winch truck fixed so that the next day they could pull the big yuccas out of the ground. Wayne has done this by hand before, but it takes too long that way to make it profitable. With the winch, the cacti come out easily, and he and J. W. can gather a truckload in a day's time. They brought a box of food to the house in the early evening, and we ate a good Sunday dinner of beans, bread, and potato salad, which Mrs. Babb served hot with onion, bacon rind, and sweet pickles.

After dinner, we gathered in the living room, Mrs. Babb sitting quietly in her chair and Wayne on the couch. Neither of them fidgeted or moved much unless they were talking. There is a complete absence of nervous gestures with both of them. J. W. had a pair of Levis on his lap. From his pants pocket, he had taken a small, neat sewing kit which held two spools of thread—white and black—a small pair of scissors, several needles, and even a thimble. He began sewing a patch on his Levis with a precise, even casting stitch. The gas heater was on, and even though the back part of the house was very chilly, the living room was warm. The two boys were outside, talking with each other on the porch and playing with the little dogs. The house was very quiet. Mrs. Babb doesn't believe in having the distraction of television or radio. She believes it is very bad for the nervous system. Once she told me: "Television makes me sick. People who look at TV only know what other people know. I want to know what I know. I wouldn't have them silly things here." And music—unless you are making it yourself—imposes an emotional atmosphere of someone else's, causing your emotions to respond artificially. She points out how nostalgic people get in hearing old songs, and she does not think it is healthy to be drawn into reminiscing. Of music she said, "I tell these people, don't spend time looking back into the past. Start learning new things. The world is turning all the time, and we need to turn with it. When we was living below Brackettville, there used to be these dances, and the main tune then was 'Silver Bells.' They had that one, and one or two more. And they'd just play it and play it. That's all they knew how to play. I just never did like it too much. But that's how I know music is a distraction. I hear one of those tunes that was played way back yonder. Well, that makes your mind go back. Does mine. You go back to that time. I can see this man just standing in the door looking on at the dancing like I was sitting there. Just takes me back."

So in her house, there was only the mood created by the combination of people who congregated there at any particular time. There was the sound of trains going by occasionally. That evening there were the voices of the boys coming from the porch outside and the frequent yapping from the dogs. There was the soft hissing of the gas heater and the stir and breathing of our four bodies.

Earlier, Mrs. Babb had urged me to get Wayne to tell his panther story. She was obviously not only proud of her son's bravery, but also sure of the entertainment value of the story itself. So, at a lull in the general conversation, I mentioned it to him. He was not at all reluctant to tell it, and from his assurance, I assumed that this was a standard story in his repertoire and had been repeated many times. In telling the story, he crouched forward, intent, with plenty of pauses for dramatic effect. He had his hat balanced on his knee, ready to put on so that he could go out later to try to get the truck started once more before he went to bed. When he talked, he fingered the hat around the brim but didn't use his hands except to illustrate specific dimensions or directions.

The story featured a large panther which, according to the tracks he left, was missing one toe. When Wayne was about seventeen, he told me, he went off with his father and some other ranchers in search of the panther that was killing off far too much livestock in the country to be ignored. After a long hunt, which Wayne outlined step by step, building suspense as he went along, the panther was finally caught sight of. Wayne shot, but the panther took off and leapt into a deep hole where the dogs and men couldn't follow him. But it was the closest the men had come to catching the animal and Walter Babb refused to let him go. He volunteered Wayne, who was still boy-sized, to be lowered down into the hole with a rope in order to finish the animal off. There was the total dark of the hole, the rope above his head, then a sudden movement, a flash of fur and eyes, and the blast of his own shotgun going off in a reflex action which matched the panther's own, and the panther was dead. After the story ended, we all sat quietly for a minute, appreciating the image Wayne had created for us of the young boy suspended in air in the dark hole above a dying animal, his father waiting for him somewhere above.

Wayne got up to let one of his dogs into the house. Killer pranced in as soon as the door opened, apparently alert to Wayne's step. He scooped the half-Chihuahua up and sat back down on the couch with the dog in his lap, stroking it between the ears. Wayne is the youngest son. Dixie and Irvin live in other parts of Texas now, but Wayne has generally lived close to his mother. He is married to a Mexican national, but she is having trouble getting her papers in order so that she can live in the United States. They own a house in Valentine, but since his wife is currently in Mexico, Wayne prefers staying with his mother. There is a shed close to the house where he keeps his traps and hunting equipment. He also has a trunk full of arrowheads, bits of pottery, and grinding stones which he has found while out in the desert.

The rest of the evening, Wayne continued to talk about hunting. "The best way to train a young dog," he said, "is to put him with an old dog that already knows how. Take them out and let him, you know, train the young one. If you don't, then you start out with a young dog. Go out and catch the bobcats in a trap, you know, and let him fight them. The more he fights them, the better he'll like it. No matter how hard they catch him by the lip or ears, the madder he gets. He hollers and howls. The ol' cat gets him by the ear, you know, blood a-flying, and that dog'll go hollering. But when he gets loose, boy, he'll go after it again. So that's the best way. You can even wet the cat with water so he can trail it real good. Then turn the cat loose. And then turn the dogs loose. Then when they get used to cat, you get 'em off on panther. Panther's a little easier for them to trail. I guess it's more scent."

Mrs. Babb sat quietly during the discussion. In prior conversations, she had told me of her dislike of both guns and dogs, but she gave no indication of these feelings in front of Wayne. At nine o'clock, she began to put the pallet down for the younger boys, signaling her own desire to go to bed. Wayne and J. W. took leave of us to sleep out in the desert so that they could run their trap line early in the morning. Mrs. Babb would have their breakfast ready the next day when they hauled the carcasses in.

CHAPTER 6

Changing Circumstances

Narrated by Jewel Babb

MR. BABB one time had five hundred sections of land, but when I married Walter, he was down to two hundred. And then it was split up, as he had several sons. So we sold our ranch outside of Langtry and came on out here. Well, we had so many kids, and we thought we might be able to spread out a little more, get the kids places. We just had a sixteen-section ranch down there. The kids always stayed with us, and so we were going to get some place so they could have a ranch. But this country is so sorry and so different from ours that we just lost everything. Goats and sheep died just like I don't know what. We didn't know how to handle them out here.

So we decided to buy this tourist court in Sierra Blanca. We had Azalea, this daughter, and she had to go to school. So when we first come here, we rented a house right on the highway. But it wasn't big enough for the family. We had four children. Dixie was married with his wife. That's before they had any children. And then Irvin was married. He had three children. Well, there was Azalea and there was Wayne, and of course us, and we couldn't get a house big enough. So Dixie went and built the tie house and lived in that. And I thought if we could just get some kind of place where we could live and be making money on the side, then we'd just do that.

The courts were small. There was about thirteen rooms. Course I added some to it. Walter was mostly out at the ranch we had. Oh, he'd come in for a while until all the people made him nervous, but then he'd go on back out again. And I had to wash clothes and make up beds and everything pertaining to a tourist court. It was pretty hard work. All day long. Because that's when the soldiers was coming back. And they'd just come in there, come and come, and I'd have to stay up all night. I'd have to get up and make beds. Make up one bed, clean up one room, three times, sometimes, in one night.

It'd just go on and on and on. And then the next morning ironing sheets. Hurts me now to look at a tourist court. They're good money, but hard work.

We didn't have enough bedding, so every time I had a few hours off in the evening, I'd get sacks. You couldn't buy material, you know, and I'd get flour sacks, just anything, and make up a quilt. It would be heavy, but I would put it on the beds. And one time—it was the coldest time we had—and I'd spent all day in the washroom washing and ironing. So that night, it was snowing and freezing and all the rooms was filled up. And one man came from Presidio asking for a room, and I said, "I don't have any more, just the washroom." And he said, "Well, I'll sleep in it." Well, I had a bed in it. So next morning, he got up, and he said, "I want to say one thing, that's the hottest room I ever slept in." I laughed. I saw him after that, and he was still laughing about it.

But flocks of soldiers would come in. They wasn't any trouble. They was all so anxious to get back home. I guess I was at the tourist courts for about eight years before I went on out to the hot springs.

Dixie had bought the Indian Hot Springs because it was adjoining our land. The hotel was there and bathhouses and a row of cabins on the hill. But the springs were in bad shape. But we was just ranch people and we just thought of it as another house, another place to live. The man who had it before was Mr. Foster. He had it for fifteen years. He had owned it longer than anybody. Because it cured his wife who had been sick years ago, he had bought it. But it was a corporation that built the hotel. They had wall-to-wall carpeting. It was fine. And they had doctors, and so many people come that all the houses was full and they had to have tents. Everywhere and up in front of it, they had tents to stay in. But when the doctors left, well, then the people left.

And Mr. Foster's wife—well, you see, this hotel was built fine, not for the poor people. And I guess she must have been a good woman because she said, "Now you just build a place for these poor people, too." So he built a row of sixteen cabins out up a ways from the hotel. Just simple rock cabins. The baths was just fifty cents and a dollar. When I moved out there, Mr. Foster was living in El Paso. But he was down there lots and lots of times. And he told me one time, "You know more about the springs than anybody that's ever been here."

So I said, "Well, nobody has ever been as desperate for money as I am." I wanted to pay for it, see. And I nearly did!

But when Dixie bought it from him, we weren't thinking of the springs at all. I'd heard about the springs, but I didn't believe it. So we had it, I don't know how many months, when a man came from Mexico City, and his wife had some kind of itch on her legs and her feet. So they came to take a bath. And so I says, "Well, there it is, go ahead and take a bath." So she did, and in four or five days, she came and she showed me how she was healed. So then I began to take notice. And other people came, and I'd talk to them. And they'd heal, too, all the sores, all the sickness, all gone, too. They'd come and I'd tell them, "Well, there it is, go on and use it."

By that time, I needed a way to make some money, so I began to look into it. I got so poor I decided, well, I needed to do something. So I got to checking. And every person that came, I talked to them. What they done, how it felt, just everything. Asked them all kinds of questions. And everything started tying in.

About the time I moved out there, Walter went to Mexico to trap some lions, way back over there close to Torreón. He loved to trap, and there was some big panther over there. He had heart trouble, see, and he wanted to get away from all this. He never did like people. Never did like to be around them. So he thought, if he got over there, he might get better. He had angina. So he went over there, and he died there. I heard it by telegram. He knew he was sick, and I did, too. He was buried in Mexico.

He had been a good man. A good worker. And he always could make money where nobody else could. He was sure a good worker. He never got hurt til he was about forty years old, and then a horse stepped in a hole and the saddle horn hit him right here.[1] Taken a long time for him to get all right. Then he got all right, but it started hurting again when he was about sixty years old. Caused obstruction and heart trouble. If I knew then what I know now, it wouldn't have been nothing. So when he'd get nervous, it'd tighten up all these vessels leading into the heart, and he'd have a heart attack. But it was about fifteen years after the injury that it started bothering him.

And then a while after we moved down to the springs, my boys got mixed up in cattle smuggling. I always will think that Walter and I sheltered them all their lives too much, so that when they did get out among people, they thought all men were honest. Irvin and Wayne were sent to jail for three years. Dixie was advised by his lawyer to go into Mexico, which he did. He was down there ten years. That left me alone, since by this time, we'd lost most everything.

When the boys left, our sheep died like flies. It was a dry spring, and there wasn't much vegetation. So, soon, I had nothing. The hotel and buildings were terribly run down. I even lost my car. But I did have a little land left that joined to the springs. So there I was with no car. I did have an old telephone that worked part of the time. I was thirty miles from a town and no money to buy but a few groceries once in a while. And the friends I thought we had run like greased lightning (as they say). The friends I had left could be counted on one hand. A woman from Oklahoma City would bring clothes that I needed. My banker that I had known in Del Rio stayed with me as long as he could. Then another friend would bring mail and groceries when he could.

I was in such desperate straits that I knew I had to learn and know what I could of the curing spring waters. I would have a few sick people now and then, but not enough to pay much. And when they did pay me any money, I'd use a part to pay for a little improvement, but the rest went for groceries. The Mexican people in Ojos Calientes[2] would bring me groceries as they could spare them. I'd go to the bathhouse to help some sick person with the baths. Then I'd come back to the hotel kitchen, and there on the table would be half a cup of coffee, a cup of flour, a cup of beans, and other little things they had to spare, as they weren't that far from starving themselves.

I had some good neighbors across the river. Valenzela[3] used to work for me, you know, help me there at the house. She worked there under the doctors, long years ago. A smart woman. She knew a lot about the springs. Oh, it was a big thing, years ago. Valenzela helped me at the springs, cook and clean up the house. When I was busy and wouldn't eat, here she'd come with a plate of food and she'd say, "Now you sit down and eat this." And she'd stay there til I did, too. She may be older than me, I don't know. Anyhow, she's part Indian. She doesn't have any family. And she raised an afflicted boy. He's just kind of crazy. I think she's still got him.

Also Juan Rivas. He's seen a lot more than I have. He was a lackey. He could fix all the pipes, electricity, cement, carpenter, he was just all-around. If a pipeline got stopped up, Juan could fix it. And this Juan, he'd come to the bank of the river, right to the edge of the water, and he'd cut up wood for me, and he'd bring it and put it on my back porch. I'd get up in the morning, and there it'd be.

Also, when the old telephone line would get mixed up in a bush or wind blow it down, he would walk it the nearly six miles at night to the main pole and fix it. He was from Mexico and was afraid officers would catch him in the daytime. So the next morning, the telephone was back in shape and ringing.

He had a good eye for officers. One time, I looked out the road and saw this rancher coming. He had a rancher's hat, and he was just dressed as a rancher. And Juan stepped outside the house. He looked. He said, "No, that's an officer." And sure enough it was. And Juan was up and gone. He'd come into the hotel and wouldn't sit down. Be looking around all the time, making sure there wasn't any immigration. One day, he saw the immigration coming and he took off across the river and fell in the middle of it and broke his leg. The bone sticking out and everything. They took him to Juárez, I guess, and cut off his leg. He has a cork one now.

But he sure helped me when I didn't have nothing and no way of getting anything. The Mexicans all were good to me, and I love them all. Good neighbors. And there was this one old man, we knew him a long, long time. About forty years I guess we'd known him. He worked for us that long. His name was Bacho. And he had a good heart, too, and would help me with the sick ones that come to the springs. Like this one. He was an old black man who had been brought over there from Odessa. And he couldn't even straighten up, he was just doubled up like a hunchback. So when they brought him out there, he came up the steps and he couldn't raise up. And he got to me and held out his hand, and he said, "Mrs. Babb, more than anything in the world, I'd like to be able to stand straight and shake a man's hand."

So in a few days he was getting better. So I would tell Bacho to go down to this spring, get a board, and when that old man got out of the bath to let him lay on this board. So he would motion to me when the old man got on the board, and I would tell him when to get off. That was done to straighten him out. And then in a few days he got fixed. The waters relaxed him, relaxed those muscles in his shoulders where the hump was. And then maybe there was a deposit there of some sort, and the waters purged it away. I think so. Because where did it go? If it didn't go in the system, where did it go? Maybe the muscles there were all pulled up and caused a collection of other poisons and things. I just don't know.

But, anyway, he had heart trouble, too. And when he come he didn't tell me that. So one day I saw him lying in bed, and since Walter had had heart trouble, I knew what it looked like. Some way that he would always prop himself up when he was lying in bed. I don't know if this is always an indication of heart trouble, but that's the way my husband was. So when I saw him laying there in this position, I said, "You have heart trouble, haven't you?" He had brought heart medicine with him, because of this heart problem, too. But he wouldn't take it once he got there. And I had told him to take his medicine and he said, "No, I won't take it til Thursday." And you couldn't make him either. So he went and taken all that medicine he had when it was Thursday. And so he got sick.

And Bacho, he came and set by that old man's bed all night. Well, I was tired and couldn't set up with him. But I'd get up at night and look out there, and Bacho setting right there by his bed. Well, he got well, and later he takened himself to his doctor and the doctor said, "Well, what I'd like to know—where is that hump?" The hump was gone. He'd been at the spring about ten days.

So that's the way that Bacho always was, helping me there at the springs. He was about sixty or sixty-five years old at the time. And he'd lived in that little village nearly all his life.

So more and more sick people began to come. I've always had a feeling for the sick, and since my young days have wanted to do all I could for them. Animals, too. I'd set up at night many times with sick animals trying to help them. But this was different. People were brought there, and they would say doctors could not help them anymore. And the little experience I'd had with sickness, I just did not know what to do with them. I'd always been close to a town or had a car where I could go get to a doctor. But here I was, no car to take them out to town, no help anywhere. I was so scared and hurt that I'd go off and cry. And I said, "Lord, now you put me down here with these people. Now show me what to do with them or how to help get them well." So I just went to God for help, and I'd do what I could for each and every one that came down for the baths.

I'd talk each day to the people that were taking baths, ask them how they felt, each and every person questioned each day. And I kept searching for something or some way to heal all the sick with baths, mosses, or the muds. And, gradually, I began to learn what each of these waters and the muds and mosses would do. I also questioned all the old-timers I could about what they knew of the spring and what cured or helped. I kept this up for the eight years I was there.

First of all, I learned that Indian Hot Springs is a shrine. And that there is a curse against the place. Somewhere or time long ago, it wasn't used right. Mr. Foster thought that, too. Rich men would buy it. Build it up. And at first, paying guests would come. Then, in a few years, it would die again. This was a pattern for many years. If it wasn't used for everybody, from the poor that are not able to pay for the baths to the very rich, whoever owns it, then something will happen to them. Seems they will die or some bad trouble come to them. This curse came from the Indians, because the springs were abused so by the white men. One time many years ago, a great deal of land was bought from the Indians by ranchers. They took these infected blankets from the smallpox camps in El Paso and traded them to the Indians for the land. Then when the Indians got sick, they all came to the springs so they could be cured. But they would bathe in the springs, then come out of the water and hit the cold air, and so hundreds of them died like flies right there around the springs. So after that, the Indians covered up the springs so the white men would not use them, and they put a curse on this water.[4] Dixie and Valenzela and I uncovered three of the springs. They are very vital if used right.

And now all around in the hills here you can see these lights, up around the springs in the mountains. Everybody sees them around here.[5] So these lights are the Indian spirits who died unnatural deaths in this country.[6] They're all around there at the springs.

But I didn't know any of that at first. First time I ever saw the lights was when a bunch of us went off, and coming back, the hotel that night was lit up completely. We was staying in the cabins. And in the hotel we had shades, those big heavy shades that were pulled down plumb to the bottom when we left. We came home that night, and that hotel was lit up like there was a person in every room, and the shades were drawn just halfway. And just as we got close, the lights went back off. The next morning, I went over there and every shade was pulled down just like I had it.

I didn't think too much of it, though, at the time. But, later, I began seeing more lights and hearing about these things. I believe lots of people saw different things while staying there. Some of them told me about what they saw. Others didn't dare mention it, as they would have been laughed at. So there was never too much talk of the unusual things they saw or heard there at Indian Hot Springs. But here is just a few of the stories I remember.

THE RUNNING HORSES

One evening, a man came to Indian Hot Springs to take the baths. He had planned to stay at least ten days. I had no rooms ready in the hotel, so fixed him up a room at the cabin on the hill. When night came and he had his supper, Wayne takened him up to his room. Some time in the night, he was awakened by a big herd, it seemed, of horses running by his door. He opened his eyes, and there stood a man looking in the screen door at him. Said this man had a funny looking hat on, also strange clothes, and seemed to be dark skinned. So he told him to go away and let him alone. The man disappeared, and so the sick man went back to sleep. Again, there was the noise of running horses, and as he looked again toward the screen door, there stood the dark-skinned man. This time, the sick man was mad and gave the man looking in the screen door a good cussing. And again told him to leave and let him alone. Then, after the dark-skinned man had left the second time, the sick man this time was wide awake and thought, "This is no man," and began to get real scared. He got up, put his shoes on, grabbed his clothes, and came down to the hotel porch fast as he could. When he come onto the porch, he was trying to get in bed with Wayne and was so scared he was talking real loud. I got up and dressed. Then went out on the porch.

I said, "What is the matter?"

He said, "Them Mexicans won't let me sleep, so I come on down here fast as I could. Because I was afraid of being killed. No telling how many Mexicans there were, I heard so many horses."

Next morning real early I went up to his room to look about for all the horses he said had passed his door. There were no horse tracks, only those of the sick man as he ran down the hill.

THE RED LIGHT VALLEY CAMPFIRE

One evening just after dark, a friend coming from Sierra Blanca drove up to the house. Some of the family and myself went out to his car to meet him. I looked on back the road he'd just come over, and there were car lights one-half mile away.

I said, "Who is coming behind you?"

He got out and also looked back.

I said, "They've had a flat, as the car is not moving. We must go see what's the matter."

He said, "Get in this car, and I'll take you over there and show you that's no car."

I got in the car, and we started back to see about the light. We drove nearly to where the light should have been, but no light or anything there. As there was no place to turn around, we crossed a deep little draw, went up on the other side. And as we got to the highest point, I looked down in a deep little gully. And there was a big campfire, flames maybe two feet high. And there seemed to be outlines of men setting around this fire. But it seemed only seconds, and all was gone, leaving only silence and the evening's darkness. And my hair standing straight up on my head.

THE LIGHT THAT SAVED THE BEGGAR'S LIFE

Once at the Indian Hot Springs, a Mexican man came to the hotel door begging for something to eat. His clothes were torn to shreds. He had no shoes, and his feet were blistered and bleeding. He'd walked for days. And as he neared the Rio Grande and was in a big deep canyon, it come up a big storm. Rain fell in sheets to where he could not see his way. And no shelter. And there was no way of knowing where to go, as it was night and he could not see. So as he was about to give up, he said, there appeared a light at his feet, and it seemed to go slowly in front of him. So he began following it until after a short ways this light went into a small cave well above the canyon floor. Said the little cave was well lit, and he could go in and be dry and safe from the raging elements.

THE INDIAN ARROWS

My friend was staying at the hotel. Taking baths and drinking the water. I had to go out to town for the day and did not get back until the next morning. She had not been scared to stay there alone. Said she sat up late that night. When she was ready to go to bed, she started down the hall. It was very dark, as in those days there were no lights down there. As she got down the dark hall a ways, a little light appeared on the floor in front of her and kept on moving down the hall. She kept on following it, thought maybe it would light the way to her room. But, no, before it got to her room, it turned into another room where she had some of her belongings. Among the things she had on the bed was a pile of arrowheads Wayne had given her. The little light went right on up on the bed and stopped with its light on all around these Indian arrowheads.

THE LIGHT ON THE WALL

One time I had two elderly men come to the springs from Beaumont. The eldest was very sick, while the youngest was not. They takened baths and drank the water each day until the night of the sixth day.

About eleven o'clock that night the younger man came dashing down to the hotel and said, "My partner is dying—come quick!"

I grabbed my coat and went out into the darkness of the night to their cabin on the hill. When I opened the door and went into his room, there he lay with his eyes fixed on the wall. I said, "What's the matter?"

He said, "I'm dying."

I said, "Why do you think so?"

He said, "See that light on the wall? It means I'm going to die."

I looked but could see no light. But his mind was made up. I got a chair and sat close to his bed and talked to him. Finally he quieted down and I left. Next morning he was feeling better and was ready to stay four more days. Which they did.

THE RECORDS

A man was taking baths at the springs and had been there for about five days. One morning he came to me and said, "You know, I had a funny thing happen to me last night. I had been asleep. When I awoke and opened my eyes, there stood a man at the foot of my bed. I could not see his face or body clearly. But only his hands. On the foot of my bed there lay two big thick books. His hands were on these books. He pushed one book aside while saying, 'This is a record of all the people these sacred waters have healed in the past.'

"Then his hands were opening the other book while saying, 'This book is to record all of the healings that will come in the future.'"

THE MAN WHO COULD SEE INTO ANOTHER LIFE

One evening at dark, two elderly men—one had his wife and daughter—came to the hotel at the Indian Hot Springs. It was late, and since they were very tired, they wanted to go to their rooms. The oldest decided he wanted a room in the hotel, while the other brother and family wanted a room in the cabin farther on up the hill. I walked down the hall with them to show the eldest brother his room. Meantime, the other brother came back to me and said, "My brother is crazy."

Anyway, they get settled, and I went to bed. Next morning, they'd all gone to take a bath before I got up. Finally, when I went into the dining room, the oldest brother came in from the bathhouse. I got him a cup of coffee, and we both sat down at the dining table to drink our coffee.

He said, "Mrs. Babb, I want to tell you what has happened to me. Doctors and people say I'm crazy." One night, he said, he went to bed. And as he closed his eyes, said he began to see people, white people. They had sores on their body, blood up to their elbows, and on their hands, and they were mean looking. They would come close to him, and he would scream and cry out. Then here comes the nurses or attendants of this hotel, and since he was in such a shape and talking to something they could not see, they rushed him to the hospital and tried to find out what was the matter with him. This happened many times.

Then he said, "Last night I saw big, strong, dark-skinned people and they were kind to me." There were no Mexican people that he could have seen that night, as every one of them had left the hotel before these people came. The girl that slept in the next room came to me after this old brother had gone to his room to rest and said, "That old man talked all night. I'd like another room."

I did not talk to him again that day. But all day I thought of what he'd told me. He was such a nice smart old man. Then when night came and we'd all gone to bed, I could not sleep. Finally, I heard his door open and the door to the restroom. We had no lights in those days, just coal oil lamps, and since he could not see good, I did not see how he could light the lamp. I soon heard the restroom's door open, and he came up the hall and opened the door to his room, then shut the door. All was quiet for a while. Then he started talking. I got up, put my housecoat on, and started down the hall. When I got to his door, I said, "Mr. Dicky, are you all right?"

After a few seconds, he said, "Yes, I'm okay, if these people would only let me alone." He said a small, dark-skinned girl was setting in the window, and others were on the dresser. While some more sat on the foot of his bed. He said, finally, he wanted to go to the restroom. But he did not know where the door was and couldn't see. Then there appeared, one on either side of him, two big, dark-skinned men. They went on either side of him to the restroom. He opened the door and went in. They were still with him. When he was ready to go back to his room, they directed him back through his door to his bed. And as he stretched out on his bed, I came to his door. He said all the dark-skinned people seemed to go down into the floor and leave.

I said, "Tell me everything you see."

He said, "Well, I see people just like us. They are working at different things, living nearly like us. I see their animals, dogs, and chickens."

THE SPIRIT DOG OF INDIAN HOT SPRINGS

One evening when it was nearly dark, I was standing by the big Bath Spring. When I looked up, here comes a big white dog trotting toward me. I thought, "What a pretty animal. I'll get him to come to me and keep him."

I began to call to him. But the dog took no notice of me, just trotted on by and kept on going until he was out of sight. I went back into the bathhouse for a few minutes. When I came out again, there was this dog again. Only this time, it was going toward the hotel.

I thought, "Now I'll run back to the hotel kitchen to get some bread and maybe catch him."

So I run fast as I could behind the dog. But he went to the back part of the hotel, and I went in the front door nearer to the kitchen. As I got the bread and went out the back door to find the dog, he was nowhere in sight. I was outside and I stood looking. When finally I saw him going in back of another house, trotting up toward the mountain, I was calling to him all this time, but it never turned its head. So again, I was running and calling to the dog. Finally, an old man that was camped up toward where the dog was going came meeting me. The dog was only about ten feet between the old man and myself in plain sight now.

He said, "What is the matter with you?"

I said, "I'm trying to catch that dog."

He stopped and looked all around, then said, "*What dog?*"

Just then the dog disappeared and I never saw him again.

THE STRANGE BEGGAR

Many years ago when Dixie bought the springs, many different times strange men would walk up to the door. Some were regular while others were tiny. They did not scare me too much, as after the First World War when I was young and living on an isolated ranch, at times there, too, were men of all kinds. Funny looking. Their clothes were different also. They would walk up to the door and ask for something to eat. They were always given a good meal. Then when they'd finish eating, they'd pull out a pocketbook and hand my mother-in-law money for their meals. But it was money that we did not know. Finally, we found out that they were German spies, coming out of Mexico into the United States.

But the men that would come to the springs were different. They had no money. No pocket book. No I.D. card or such. I never treated them too good at first, because I thought they were spies, too. Not until the time a very little person walked up to the door. It was raining and freezing, wintertime. We asked him inside. Then, as he sat down, we saw he had only the thinnest of clothes. But he held some kind of jacket and he tried to keep his arms covered with it. We were asking him all kinds of questions. I said to him, "Who sent you here?"

He looked straight at me, with the most beautiful dark eyes I've ever seen, and said, "My boss."

We talked a while longer. I got up and said, "You can sleep in this room; the bed is ready."

At that he pulled away the jacket from his arms. And I saw that the middle of each arm doubled back at the elbow, making from the elbow to the hand a U-shape, both arms the same way. I knew then that he was very special. When I got up to leave, he said, "I wish I could pay you, but you'll be paid in other ways." I went on out. Next morning, the bed had not been slept on and he was gone.

CHAPTER 7

The Hot Springs

Narrated by Jewel Babb

I KEPT ON working with all the sick that came there. White people. Mexicans. Negroes. Creoles. Cajuns. Sometimes there would be people setting on the porch. One group would be talking Spanish, and over on another part they would be talking French. Sometimes when they'd feel better after taking baths for a week, we'd all get together and walk out over the hills looking for pretty rocks. I'd look at them and think, all of us get along so well down here. Now why can't nations get along and not be fighting all the time? After all, we belong to God. He made us. And how can we think that one of us is the best race?

So I kept on learning about the waters. I learned if you take a plant from one spring and put it by another, this water'll kill it. Each one kills the other's plants. Then when one kind of hot water stopped curing. Then what spring next to go on to finish. Because if you take a bath out there in one spring water, that'll go so far and will stop. Then you have to go to another one to finish it up. So if you want to clean up your liver, this Bath Spring might go so far, but it'll take the Sulphur Spring to finish curing it.[1] I helped many people over those years and washed the feet of both white and black. I remember my old grandma and her foot baths good for so many ills. And I found it worked down there at the springs, too, only better.

I found that most all diseases was cured down there except cancer.[2] It scatters in the body when the water there stimulates the system. But I believe there is a cure there for it, too. But I never found it. And all the eight years I was there, I never stopped searching for better ways to help the sick. Of all the sick people that came there, none died from bathing or being alone down there. I even found there were certain rocks to set on and what that would do for a disease. Which waters had the alpha, beta, and gamma rays. Which was too strong to bathe in. Mr. Foster, in talking to me one time, said he had an analysis which showed that only one hot spring in the world even approached the waters of Indian Hot Springs, and that one was in Germany. And I, too, believe all the medicine you ever need is there in some of those waters.[3]

There are twenty-two springs down there, maybe more at one time. But most people now don't even know where they all are, except for the big ones. The Chief Spring is the one that was built over the old Indian rock bath. Sometimes we call it the Bath Spring, too. It's a rock bathhouse with tiled bathtubs, a lounge with a fireplace, and massage tables. Water is piped into the bathtubs from the spring. So you start any cure with regular baths and drinking the water regular from the Bath Spring. You start with one, maybe two glasses, on the first day, and work up to about a gallon a day. This clears out the body of all the poisons in the system. Purges you.[4] One thing about that spring, though. You take baths a couple of days, and you feel real good. You keep on taking the baths, and first thing you know, you're sick as a dog. And that's when you say you're going to give it up. It treats you bad before it treats you good. I think it gets to stirring you all up, and then that's when you go to cussing the springs. There's always a purge. But you keep on bathing and drinking and keep on purging all the bad stuff out of your system; then in a few days you're feeling real good.

But it's good for other things, too. Heart trouble. You bathe in it and drink the waters. Tuberculosis, too. Any kind of lung diseases. For that, you need to sit on the side of the spring and breathe in the fumes of it.[5] After so long, you start sweating, right along in the chest area.

Then there's the Squaw Spring. And it's good for all kinds of female ailments. It's too strong to drink, though, but it's good to bathe in. And it helps the fertility.[6]

Then right above the hotel is the Soda Spring. It's covered with a cement slab and the water's piped directly into the hotel. But it's medicine water, too. Good drinking water, good for digestion. It don't purge.[7]

Then there's Stump Spring, which is along the river down from the Squaw Spring. Valenzela helped me dig this one up. Really it's two springs, one hot and one cold. The hot one is radioactive. Radium, thorium, and uranium.[8] The Bath Spring has just a little. But it's mostly this one. There's certain rocks you sit on, and the funniest thing, if you have a bad hip or anywhere that you have a bad spot on your bone, you set on this rock and directly you feel something going up your toes and on up the top of your head, turns around and comes down. But first it might stop and work on that bad place.

This Stump Spring is good, too, for diabetes. You can drink a little bit but not much, though, because it's too strong. But you bathe in it. So you can eat anything you want to. I don't know whether it'll cure completely or not, but all the time you're there you could eat just anything.[9] And then this Stump Spring is also good for asthma, too.

Then there's another pair of hot and cold springs up in the canyon area a little ways away from the river. This one isn't marked, though. It's a mud spring with gray mud. It's about two foot underground, and you go in there and you set down. And over here is a tiny hot springs, and over here is a cold one. So you sit there, and you smear yourself with all that mud, and if you have a problem with sleep, afterward when you go back, you'll just sleep and sleep and sleep. And if you have sores on you, it'll take those sores off you right then. The next day you might have a place there that looks like when you have an open sore which the sun has got to and dried up. That's what it looks like.

Then there's the Sulphur Spring. And that sulphur mud is the best thing. Good for acne and sores. And it's good for your complexion, too. This man come one time, and he was talking about the mud, and I said, "Just get your hat and show me where it is." Sulphur mud. It's coal black and you take it out. Be sure to get no gravel and no rocks, and if you do, take them out with a sifter. It's just like Pond's Cold Cream except it's just as black as ink. Smear it on your face and keep it there til it dries and then you wash your face.[10]

Then on top of these springs are these mud mosses. But the Health Department came out some time not long ago and made Mr. Hunt clean them out. They claimed a health hazard. That's because they didn't know any better. But those mosses are the most curative things. I'd take those mosses and make packs out of them and lay them on your body and let them stay there a little while until they get dry. I've used them on people and horses both for broken bones and wounds.[11]

I sure saw a lot of people get well. There was one woman with a black leg who came to the spring. Some men from over in Odessa brought her. She had phlebitis. Blood clots. Her foot was all right, but not the lower part of her leg. It looked like someone had takened a butcher knife and cut all the flesh off to the bone and the bone itself was black. Well, I run water over her leg. Seventeen days of hot water from the Bath Spring, black mud and moss from the Sulphur Spring. And every day it grew a little more like life was coming back in it. She said the moss was like a million needles sticking all over her leg. Then one day all these people were taking naps on the porch, and this woman was in a chair. She hadn't been walking at all before this. I said, "Get up." When she got up, something funny feeling, she said, was at the top of her head; then when she got up, it went away. And there she was, walking again on that leg.

One time a man came there to bathe. Nearly all of his skin was gone. He had to be wrapped in soft blankets, and he kept his body greased with some kind of oil. After the second bath, his body was dried. And it looked as if the sun or something had burned him just a bit. Not enough to hurt. But it was a funny look. I had a big black German shepherd there, and the kids had learned him to pick up rocks and take them and try to give them to people. And if you didn't take the rock, he would drop it at your feet. After six or seven days, this man began to get outside without his oil and blankets and walk around. One day I went to see him. First thing he said was, "Damn the dog and damn the flies!" It was summertime, and there were lots of flies. And he said the dog came to see him when he got out and kept bringing rocks and dropping them on his toes.

Two men came once from Beaumont. They'd never seen a high mountain. They came down the road, and at their first look from high up on the mountains, they stopped their car on a level place in the road to look down at the hotel. One of them said, "I believe that's the place. But how are we going to get down?" Finally, they did drive up to the hotel. They takened a cabin on the hill and began their baths. The fifth day after dark, one came down to the hotel and said, "Come quick. My partner is dying." Then without waiting for me, he went back. I walked up the hill to their cabin in the dark. There he lay, and, to my eyes, he looked like he was about to die. I sat down by his bed and talked to him. Finally, though, I decided he'd drunk so much of the purgative water and had not eaten a thing all day, that it was hunger more than anything else. So I went down to the hotel and brought up a can of beef soup. And I heated the soup in the kitchen of the cabin. When it was ready, I takened it to him. He ate the whole can of it. Then I stayed there with them for maybe half an hour, talking to him. Finally, when he had food in his stomach, he was all right again.

Then there was a woman who brought her husband there at two

o'clock in the morning, drunk. She drove up to the front of the hotel, and as I stood in the front door of the porch, she said, "Here is my husband. See that he don't drink any more." And she drove off. He came staggering up the walk. Wayne was there with me by then. We had a bad time with this one. Wayne was giving him baths. And the man was getting drinks from across the river where they could always make tequilla out of sotol bushes. So it was a lost cause.

Some people brought a tiny Negro girl there once with some terrible scalp disease. Her head was shaved. After so many hot water baths, I put her in the mud bath. I had to get down in the mud with her. I'd put the mud all over her head. And if I looked at her, she stuck her tongue out at me. But she would never say a word. In a week or so, all this scalp disease was gone, and the skin on her head was clear and healthy.

Then there was a woman that weighed over three hundred pounds. Her husband had left her because she was nearly helpless. She could not set down in an ordinary chair. We had to get one more than extra big. She'd set there and go to sleep. She began her baths and drinking the water. In twenty days, she'd lost so much weight that she could put her girdle on. And in all my life, I have never seen a person so tickled. She went back home and got herself a good babysetting job.

Polio cripples also came. I'd work with them, helping them bathe, and in a few days the muscles did turn loose, and the only thing left of the crippled legs was the habit of limping. That would take longer to get rid of. I reported these healings to doctors in the polio wards and asked them to bring a polio cripple or send one down for baths and I'd help and there would be no charges. And I was written back, "There is no such thing. We doctors have put all together [reckon he meant minerals and hot water baths] and it won't work. We are not interested."

A young man very sick with TB came. He told me he had a very bad case of asthma. Nothing about having TB. But I noticed when he spit on the ground, he always takened his foot and covered it up with dirt. He would take a hot bath and sweat, and he always told me, "I sweat most of all on my chest." He stayed and takened baths a good many weeks and he did get better.

Sometimes there would be as many as fifteen people there at one time with different kinds of disease. Since we had many rooms, there was plenty of places for each and every person to stay. Some had little hot plates where they could prepare their own meals, while others shared the main kitchen. Every single person brought their own groceries. One or two even hired a small trailer and brought groceries. They would be prepared to stay ten days or more.

I did not cook too much. Valenzela takened care of most all the meals. Then, also, some of the women staying there would cook. Valenzela knew when she saw me leaving with someone to the bathhouse she'd better hurry to the kitchen, as probably I'd put something on to cook, and when someone needed a bath, everything else would be forgotten, and the pan itself would burn up.

Sometimes there would be famous people come there, musicians and so on. They would go to the old piano in the evening and start playing. And before they'd start, the Negro people would be setting together in one part of the lobby, while the white people would be in the other part. After the wonderful music began, a Negro woman would get up and go stand at the piano and start singing. Then a white man would get up. Together the two would sing, and their voices were out of this world. Pretty soon, race was forgotten, and all had moved up closer and were standing together singing or listening. There was one woman who came quite often. When she came in the door, the first thing she did was go to the piano and start playing *The Old Rugged Cross*. I knew that one was for me.

At times when I was without money, someone from Sierra Blanca or the vicinity would come and pay me to let them have a dance and barbecue in the hotel. Some of them would get a little wild, as there would be plenty to drink from both sides of the border, and if the people across the river were having a dance at the same time, things really got loud. Singing from over in Mexico, music, loud talk, and finally, toward morning, fights would break out, and pretty soon they'd start bringing the wounded over to get someone to take them to the doctor. Their shirts would be bloody and torn. Then the doctors reported to the police, and most of the wounded would land up in jail. Most all the time, Agustín T. would play for these dances in the hotel, and the dance would go on well into the morning, or until everyone was so tired and sleepy they could not go on.

One time I had a woman there who would get very drunk. Sometimes she would try to go outside, make it out the door, and fall down. And I'd go out to help her up and back to her room. One day a preacher came to preach to the people on the other side. He and his wife came on into the hotel. And about that time, the woman began to scream. The preacher stopped and said, "What's that?" I said, "Oh, it's a woman that's had a little too much to drink." After that, he was in a big hurry to leave.

One evening I was alone at the springs. I'd gone up to the cabins on the hill to clean them up. Wayne had brought another big load of old ties and lumber, and it had been stacked up on some rocks and the ties between the hotel and cabins. I got through with my work on the hill and came walking on back, passed this big stack of lumber, and was about to walk up on the back porch. The dogs began to bark, and I looked back to see a man crawling from out under the lumber. He was a big man. All his clothes were torn, and he was nearly naked. No hat, but long hair and a beard. He was coming toward me, but he seemed not to see me. Just looking at the dogs. When the dogs got close to him, between me and this wild crazy man, they began to try to stop him. He grabbed up a rock nearby as big as a person's head, but didn't throw it at them. Just held it in his hands above his head ready to try and kill them with it if they got closer. His eyes seemed to me big as saucers, and I was terribly afraid. But I thought if I could just get in the hotel and lock the doors, I'd be safer. So while the dogs held him off, I did make it into the door of the hotel and latch the screen.

Strange that he never seemed to see me, although he was real close, but rather kept his eyes on the dogs. I went through the front room of the hotel and looked out at him. He was still ready to kill the dogs if they came close to him. Finally he turned away and started walking toward the bathhouse. I was afraid each minute that he'd turn and come back, but he kept going on, passed the bathhouse and went down the river. And I never did see him again.

And in those days, there were lots of Mexican officers there across the river. They'd come out of Mexico onto the United States side, then drive on down to the springs to cross back into Mexico. They'd most always get there around ten o'clock at night. They would want a room to sleep in. And if I was asleep, they'd keep on knocking until they woke me up. Lots of times I was alone in the hotel. I'd go to the door, open it, and step outside where they would be. Eight or ten standing around. I'd show them where to go and get a room ready in the cabins on the hill. I'd talk a little while to them. Then they would go on to find their room and stay all night. Then they'd cross over to Mexico the next morning. One of my friends would be there sometimes and see these men come at night. And she said, "Mrs. Babb, you are under divine protection, as you are never harmed."

Sometime later, there was a woman who came to the springs and fell in love with a Mexican *comandante* who patrolled the river. All the women up and down the river were after him, even though he was married. But then she was married, too. He spoke Spanish and she spoke English, so they got Holly[12] to act as interpreter. She had a little pair of red slippers, and, to show his love, he would kiss them ever once in a while. So, finally, they decided to get married. I told her, "Now don't go with him into Mexico. He'll put you in a house and lock up and take the key." But she went anyway. And sure enough, that's what he did. He was so jealous, he wouldn't even let her talk to a child. So one day—she was a real good cook—she had fixed a good meal and set it on this little table for the two of them. Soup and bread and honey. And he said, "Remember those little red slippers you had at the river?" Well, yes, she remembered and was so happy he asked. "Well," he says, "little red slippers like that are only worn by whores." She up-ended the table on him, and he wound up with honey down the front of his uniform. She left him shortly after that.

While I lived at the springs, the hotel and cabins were flooded out three times. The first time, Wayne had piled a lot of old heavy lumber out in front of the hotel, about forty feet from the front. I had my car parked in front of the old storeroom building. It had been raining off and on for a week. Finally, the river began to rise. It stood full from bank to bank. Then there came another real heavy shower, and as the little canyons began to run into the Rio Grande, it also began to have more water, and water began to come up close to the hotel and cabins. I kept watching as it came up, foot by foot, until it was all around the hotel, and then finally, when I saw how fast it was coming, I began moving some of my things, such as a few quilts, coffee, and some more groceries to the bathhouse, quite a distance from the hotel. Each time I came back to the hotel, the water was higher. In a few minutes, the water was up in the cabins. Then the big planks began to move off in the water in front. I kept taking things out to the bathhouse and wading back through the water to the hotel. It was late evening, and I could see the water. Then the last time I went into the hotel, I looked back, and the river had stopped rising. But it takened several hours for it to run back down. My car was in the water halfway to the top. And it was never good anymore. This time, even though the water was nearly up to the floor in the hotel, it did not seem to hurt the building. But it did ruin all the furniture in the row of cabins. The bedding was soaked. And the mattresses all had to be pulled out of the mud. The chimneys were also full of mud and silt.

The second time I was alone. I went to bed early, after seeing that my white German shepherd, Duchess, and her six puppies were safe about two hundred yards up in one of the cabins. I must have gone to sleep right away. But something woke me. I raised up and looked out the window, and all I could see was water everywhere. I jumped up quick as I could and knew I had to go get those little puppies. I grabbed a housecoat and put it on as I went through the hotel. When I stepped off the porch into the dark waters, they came up above my knees, and I walked in it as best as I could. All the two hundred yards or so was water. And very swift. I knew I had to go slow, as if I fell, I might not be able to get up again. And, too, I knew big rattlesnakes were always washed down in such waters. But by going slow and watching my feet, I made it to the cabin where the pups were. I opened the door, and the water in the cabin was up two feet or higher. I thought, oh, now the pups are gone or drowned. The mother had met me at the door, but I reckon she was so scared, she did not know what to do, as she was no help. Anyway, I looked across the room and in a corner saw some little heads bobbling around. I went over, and there were four of the little puppies. I gathered them up in my skirt. But I needed to find the other two if they weren't washed away. So I looked and looked. Finally, I went to the door that I'd come through. I pulled it back, and there were the other two. I knew I could not carry all six in my skirt front. So I saw a box on top of a table that was above the water. I got the box, put all the puppies in it, then started for the bathhouse. This time it was easier walking, as I was going with the water. But my heart was still in my mouth. But I finally made it to the bathhouse with Duchess and her family. And since the bathhouse is always warm, I stayed there the rest of the night. In the morning all the water was gone. But there was lots of damage done to the cabins and parts of the hotel.

The last time the river got up around the hotel, it was terrible and nearly got us. I had an old sick man sleeping in the front bedroom. Another lady was in the back part of the hotel. It had been raining off and on for many days. And, again, the river was full of water up to the ditch behind the hotel. As we all went to bed, I was afraid, and I knew if it come one more hard shower, no telling what the river would do. But, anyway, I went on to bed and to sleep. I don't know how long I slept. Finally, something woke me up. I raised up and looked out the window, and there was water, water everywhere as far as I could see from my window. In front of the hotel, too. I grabbed my flashlight and feather quilt. I called Duchess and started taking things that I'd need again to the bathhouse, thinking I'd get what was needed out first. Then I came back to try to get this woman and the old sick man out through the water to the bathhouse. I got to the porch, opened the screen door, and looked out. The water was swift, and my dog didn't want to step out in it. Anyway, as I went down the steps of the porch, the water got deeper and deeper. It came way up above my knees. Again, I was afraid more of rattlesnakes being in the water than I was of the water itself. But I kept on going through it. Since it was dark, I couldn't see my way too much. So I walked out too far where a lot of rocks had been piled up. I got on these rocks, slipped, and fell down in two feet of water. My feather quilt and my flashlight went down, too. When I raised up, my light was still on and shining, but my quilt was all wet. I finally made it to the bathhouse. Then I turned to go back through the water to the hotel. As I got a ways out in the water, I saw something coming through the water toward me. As I got closer and could see better, I saw it was my woman friend. She was coming out through the deep water, trying also to get to the bathhouse. But she was smarter than me. She'd picked up a broom on her way out to the bathhouse and held it as sort of a crutch to help her wade out. She had her blankets across her shoulder. I stopped and asked her if the water was up in the hotel yet. She said, no, but a few more inches of water would get up to the floor. She went on to the bathhouse, and I went back into the hotel to see about the old sick man. I got on the porch and thought I'd see how fast the water was rising. But, no, it had stopped. So I knew if the water had stopped, there was no more danger. It would run down pretty quick. So I kept quiet and did not go to wake the old man. In the morning, he said he'd seen everything through the windows. And since he knew he could not get out by himself, he had just prayed for our safety. This time, since the water had stayed up so high around the hotel so long, there was lots of damage to the building. The hotel looked like a big boat. With water all around it, in the light of my flashlight.

I had been at the springs several years before I knew that I had any power to heal with the mind. It had probably been coming on for a while, but I didn't know it. Then one day, this man came who had a very bad pain in his shoulder. He had to take strong medicine to relieve the pain. So I put moss on his shoulder. He got out of the tub, and I put the moss on his shoulder. And then when he covered up, why I stepped way across the room and I sat down. And his face was uncovered, and he knew I was over there because he could see me. Finally, he says, "Quit pressing so hard with your thumb."

Well, you can imagine how I looked. So I didn't say anything, just looked at him, because I thought he was crazy. He could see I wasn't pressing on his shoulder. So, directly he said, "Quit pressing so hard with your thumb."

His face was getting red, and I knew he was mad. So I got up and went over and pulled that mud off. And he was mad. And I just rubbed this arm just a little bit and then everything was gone. Hurt and everything.

So I wondered about that. And I went off by myself afterward away from everybody. I was praying and asking what this was that was happening. And I saw something like a vision. I saw these little men with something like flashlights. And wherever someone was sick, they'd shine their light on it. They were the prettiest men you ever saw. They have the roundest little faces, their cheeks was red, and their skin was a light gold color. And their heads were just so round, pretty hands, and then they had a band around their head, and then their light. And ever time they was going to heal anybody, then they shined that light on that person. And they weren't friendly. Later, when my mother was sick, I was thinking about her to help her, and I saw about eight of those little men come around her bed, four on one side and four on the other. They just looked at her, and then they put their hands behind their backs. There was no foolishness about them.

I never see spirits, only the doctors. I can see their hands, how they hold them and massage ever place. And I see just three different kinds. One of them was so little and such an ancient age, wrinkled all over, and had clothes that I never seen the like, and he massaged the back. This was the funniest thing—with his knees. I saw him with a man who was crippled in the war and his back was healed. Then another one was a doctor of modern times. He had long hands. I could see his hands reach plumb around from one part of the neck to the other and how he could massage the atlas and the axis part of the neck. But that's all I seen, just three doctors. Massaging and using their lights.

Well, I was learning more than I ever had. But as time went on, I knew I was going to lose the springs. Toward the last it was mostly Negroes that was coming. I charged $10.00 for ten days. Springs and room. At the end of the ten days, some would say they didn't have enough money to get home. Then I would lend the money, tell them to send it back, and they would. They came from Odessa, Midland, Beaumont, Louisiana. The Negro women were a spiritual help at the time. There was a man with rheumatism who came with his wife, and the springs really helped him. I was real worried. I told him, "Next time I probably won't be here." He said, "Well, Mrs. Babb, the Big Man has it all under control."

He helped me as much as he could. I went to Odessa in a station wagon and visited his family. He gathered up about ten old women crippled up with arthritis. And then I drove them back. I'd watch them in the bathhouse. One old woman had a chew of snuff in both jaws. I told her to spit it out so she could drink the water. But the woman said she could pack it in her jaws and still swallow. But the white people in Sierra Blanca didn't like the Negroes. And the people at the filling stations discouraged them. Discouraged everyone from going there. They would say the roads were bad and no way to get there.

So I tried to sell the springs. I put it up for sale. But I didn't have no luck there either. It's never been no good trying to make any money on those springs. One man from Mexico City wanted the springs. Said he'd go back to make the arrangements. Getting off the train, he died. Then there was a man from Albuquerque came and wanted it. When he got back to Albuquerque, he died, too. Another man from Midland said, "I'll put a Cadillac at each door." He stepped outside during a rain and broke his hip. Didn't want it none after that. And a rich man from El Paso came in a Cadillac. The Cadillac turned over on the road almost. He turned right around and went back to El Paso.

There was one time that men were supposed to come from Black River Village in New Mexico. Ministers. They sent word they were coming to see the place, as they wanted such a spot for a retreat. So I began to try to clean up the hotel for them to see. I'd gotten about two gallons of white paint, and one of the men across the river said he'd paint the big front room, the lobby of the hotel. So it takened him about three days or more to paint it. Then another man came over and helped me scrub the floor and shine up the furniture with kerosene. So the very morning the men were to come, my helper came early so that we could finish with the cleaning and have everything ready. Then, as it was wintertime and it was cold in the big lobby and we didn't have enough wood to make a fire, I told him, "Maybe we can put a car tire in the big fireplace." So right away, he went out and brought in this tire and placed it in the fireplace. It didn't take long for the tire to catch fire. At first it did fine. Then as it burned more, it also smoked more. The chimney could not carry all the smoke out of the fireplace. Smoke began pouring out into the lobby that we'd just painted white. It got worse and worse. My helper was scared, run out the back door, and got up on a ladder to see what was happening on top of the hotel. He'd look, then he'd run back down the ladder and on into the lobby to see what the fire was doing in the fireplace. But there was no fire any more, only coal black smoke. Well, by this time he was speechless, and he was a good cusser most of the time. And I was just looking at the smoke boiling out of the big fireplace. The smoke would go straight up to the ceiling and just seemed to hang there until it was a solid black cloud. And when there wasn't so much smoke coming out the chimney, there was this black smoke hanging about five and a half feet from the floor.

About that time, I looked out and saw this big car driving up. I went on out to the back porch and looked at the men. I asked them in, and they began getting out of the car, four of them, really dressed up. They came on into the kitchen, then walked on into the lobby. Three of the men were rather small. Their heads just touched the cloud of smoke. The other was a very tall man, and his head was up in the smoke so that you couldn't see his face. I thought of the headless horseman. They walked a little farther, then turned back. One of them said, "Well, we'd better be going." And they left real quick. I did not know whether to laugh or cry. The pretty room was black, and I'd missed what I thought would have been a good sale. Then I caught sight of my face in a mirror, and it was solid black except for my mouth and eyes. After that, I realized that I never would be able to sell the springs.

So after that I finally lost the springs. Years later, Mr. H. L. Hunt bought it all for back taxes from the bank in Del Rio. But he never was able to make a go of it either. He put a lot of money into it, though, trying to shape it up. He built a pen for white-tailed deer and ran cattle. Made a greenhouse for *Aloe vera.* He made more tubs in the bathhouse and installed whirlpool baths. And there behind the hotel, he built a dike along the river so that the buildings wouldn't all flood out anymore. He had a radio program in Dallas and advertised the springs on that. But there was such bad rains then. And the roads washed out. And then there doesn't seem to be so many people any more interested enough in hot springs. So they go to Truth or Consequences instead. One of these other spring places that are easier to get to. Even though none of them is near as good as these springs here are.

I always thought very highly of Mr. Hunt. The first time he came down there, his wife and him come down together. Seemed like they rented a car from El Paso. So I guess they had somebody to drive them there. Anyway, Agustín must've come every Saturday and Sunday morning to the spring. And this Sunday morning, he went there, and there was Mr. Hunt. And he says to Agustín, "Tell me about this and tell me about that." So Agustín told him he better ask me, that he didn't know anything, that he needed to talk to Mrs. Babb. And Mr. Hunt says, "That's who I want to talk to. Go get her!"

So Agustín come and he got me. And I didn't have time to iron a dress or anything. And we drove up to the hotel, and his wife come out the door, and he come out the door to see us, you know. And then we sat on the porch and he started asking questions all about the springs. And they was the nicest things, real friendly and nice. So we talked, and then when Agustín went and taken me home, Mr. Hunt says, "I'll go with you." So he gets in Agustín's old car, and we all go up to the tie house. And that's a mess, you know. But he didn't care. So we got there, and then later on Agustín taken him on back. He stayed a good long time. He asked me all kinds of questions about the springs. And I'd lost my glasses like I always do. And the tie house was so dirty I said, "Here, let's go out to the trailer and sit down." So we sat down on the trailer, and he handed me something and said, "Here, look at this."

And I said, "No, I can't see. I can't find my glasses."

And he said, "Well, here's mine."

So he'd lend me his glasses and I'd look, and then he'd want to look, and I'd hand him back his glasses. And so it went back and forth, until we got through talking.

So anyway, sometime after that, he come again. So he sent word. He sent his brother-in-law out to bring me down to the springs. So I went down there and stayed, I think, three days. So he was telling me about this hurt he had in his groin, and I said, "Well, maybe it could be controlled by your feet."

And he didn't understand that. So he goes and asks somebody, some men there, and he asks what they thought about what I said. And they said, "Well, just try it."

So I did it for him, and he liked it so well that I give him two treatments a day, one in the morning and then at nighttime I'd have to go to my room and stay until he come in and go to bed. About ten o'clock. Then I'd go there and massage his feet. At the time, I hadn't worked up too high. I knew about massaging feet, but I was still learning about how to use the mind. So I was working with his feet one night, and the light was right in his eyes. So he said, "I wish we could put something over that light. It's bothering my eyes." He said, "Put my sock over it."

So I put his sock over it. And when I was busy with his feet, directly his sock got too hot. He said, "You better take that sock off, it's gonna burn up." I would have never thought of that. So when he was there, I would stay at the hotel in one of the rooms to work on his feet. And to talk to him about the springs. He sure did like it. Well, he believed in all these natural things, like natural foods. When he was at the springs, he taken the baths, but he'd go home to Dallas and stay a good long time. I think he was only there three times. Maybe another time. I taken care of his boy, Hassie, too, who was sick. Had different things wrong with him. I taken care of him two different times.

Then another time a bunch of us were below the hotel close to the river. They looked up, and they saw a man walking to the hotel, and he had a little hand bag. And he wasn't dressed very good. So Mr. Hunt looked up and he said, "Go tell that man to come here. I want to talk to him. I might learn something." A man like that learning something from a tramp. But that was the way he was.

The last time I saw him, he said, "I have great respect for you, Mrs. Babb." People had told him so many things about the old rough woman, you know. So Mr. Hunt died not so long ago, and so far as I know, there's no one down there at the springs any more. It's vacant now. And I haven't been down there myself for a long time.

CHAPTER 8

Alone on the Rio Grande

VERY LITTLE has been written on the history of the springs, although they have apparently been used extensively, first by the Indians, later by Anglo settlers who came to the area. The first known report of the springs came from Captain Jeff Maltby, who was commissioned in 1884 by ranchers to inspect the land in the northern Rio Grande region for cattle ranching possibilities. Describing his ride into the springs area, he relates: "The old signs and trails leading into the springs indicated that the Indians held the virtues of these springs as the people of old Biblical times held the Pool of Siloam."[1] But his final opinion on the suitability of the land for settlement was negative and he reported to the ranchers that they should not waste their time in the area. The river, he wrote, was sporadic, the bandits were rampant, and bands of hostile Indians still roamed the area. In fact, only four years earlier, a scouting group of seven Negro cavalry men, after spending the night at the springs, were murdered during breakfast preparation by Apache leader Victorio and his men, who had escaped from a New Mexico reservation.

Yet, just twenty years after Captain Jeff's reconnaissance report, ranch people were in the area and visiting the springs by horse and buggy—camping between the old rock-hewn tub left by the Indians, which the springs flowed through to the Rio Grande, and the seven graves of the murdered cavalry men.

Several of the older residents of Sierra Blanca can remember the springs from the time they were young. Mrs. Dee Elliott, born and raised in Sierra Blanca, said that her mother told her about going there with a horse and buggy, bringing tents and camping equipment and staying two or three weeks for baths around 1905–1906. And Mrs. Dogie Wright, also of Sierra Blanca, could remember going as a child in a hack; her family would build a brush arbor and set up iron beds inside it, then do all the cooking over a campfire.[2] According to her husband, Dogie Wright, Sierra Blanca's local historian, the first attempt at commercializing the springs was around 1907 when someone started renting out cots and tents at the springs and set up a kitchen shack on the hill. But the first real buildings weren't constructed until 1929 when an El Paso corporation built the rock hotel along with the cabins which are still there. And on the site of the Indian rock tub, a bathhouse was erected, permanently covering the artifact. Two doctors were hired by the corporation, Dr. Caylor and Dr. Thomas, and a staff of nurses was hired to assist them. In addition to administering baths and massages, the hotel apparently operated at the time as a clinic, also. Dogie Wright recalls checking into the hotel in 1930 for kidney and bladder trouble. He was given injections and was finally operated on by Dr. Caylor. He remembers this stay as being a pleasant one; there was a full-time cook, and fresh vegetables were brought in every day from a farm on the river below. The rooms were spacious and clean, and the care was good. Even though he was too sick to take baths, he recalls that the other patients were on a daily regimen of taking baths in the mornings and relaxing in the afternoons.

But the ambitious plans for a European-style spa ultimately failed. Dogie Wright says there were several reasons. An earthquake in 1931 lowered the water, and it took a while for it to come back up to a useable level. The river also got lower, hurting the hunting and fishing which had also been a part of the springs' attraction. And the Depression itself hit almost on the heels of the major investment in construction. J. D. Foster, one of the original members of the corporation, gradually bought out the other members until he became the sole owner of the springs. Although for several years he struggled to keep it alive, his attempts became more futile, and the war years, with rationing of gasoline and austerity programs, called a halt to the commercial use of the springs.

In 1952, when Mrs. Babb first came to the springs, the hotel had been abandoned for several years, flooded periodically by the Rio Grande, and plagued with vandalism. She tried to keep it open herself for eight years before losing it for back taxes and moving to the tie house.

Although I asked Mrs. Babb several times about going to Indian Hot Springs with me, she never really wanted to go. She would say each time that she would like to but then would have reservations when the date got close to leave: she was not sure her car would make it; she was not sure my car would make it; she would have taken a turn in her health and would be feeling drained of energy; or she would need to take care of Wayne and his boys when they came in from trapping. This was characteristic of her refusal to encourage nostalgia. Writing about her past, she told me, had stirred up her mind too much as it was.

Finally, I packed up the Volkswagen myself one day to explore the springs area. I took the now-familiar left turn out of Sierra Blanca as if I were going to the tie house, but two or three miles out of town I veered right instead of left. The road was hard-packed dirt and gravel, and it was dangerous to drive more than thirty miles an hour. Mrs. Babb said this was one reason why no one has ever been able to make money on the hot springs; the access is just too difficult. The road seemed to stretch endlessly. It was in the middle of February, and the air was cold and crisp. The desert was dormant, brown and lifeless. The dust kicked up behind me in a great cloud, but the drive was pleasant in the crisp winter air. I had become comfortable with this terrain since my first trip to see Mrs. Babb more than a year ago. The road went down into gorges, then around curves and back up hills. Finally, I rounded a high curve and, looking down on my left, I could see far below me the canyon rocks flatten out into a plain with a ribbon of trees in the middle marking the Rio Grande. And in the middle of the plain was a large sprawling adobe structure with several smaller structures scattered around it. Although it was white-washed and neat, even from that distance I could tell that it was deserted.

Coming down off the mountain and onto the Rio Grande plain, it was easy to see why stories spring up about the place. I was struck by the quietness and barrenness of the grounds. There was no grass close up around the springs, just flat sand, almost like a beach, with white mineral deposits caked on the top, sloping gently to the river where the underbrush finally bushed up and out. I pulled the Volkswagon in front of the hotel. There was a group of cabins to the right of it, several hundred yards away, and to the left was a series of small shacks, each one apparently built over a hot spring. When I killed the engine, there was no other sound to replace it. The hotel was obviously locked up and its windows shuttered. If there were owners, they were not living on the grounds.

I began walking around the springs. There were small wooden signs on each one of the sites with names I had become familiar with through the long talks with Mrs. Babb. The biggest was the Chief Spring, with an enclosed bathhouse on the edge of it, which pumped its water into whirlpool baths. A few yards away was the Squaw Spring with a wooden fence around it and a wooden roof built over it. I unlatched the gate and stepped onto the stones around its side. The bubbles came up slowly and evenly paced from—what depth? According to Mrs. Babb, perhaps from the center of the earth. When I stuck a hand in, the water was warm on the surface and half a foot down even warmer, varying, according to official reports, from 100° to 118°.[3] The steam rose from it in the winter air. Several yards farther on were two small springs together, unmarked. Above them a dozen paces away was a round white swimming pool with a bathhouse—deserted and empty with tumbleweeds wafting along the bottom. From the slight elevation of the swimming pool, I could look across the river. Barely visible on the other side of the trees was a cluster of roofs and dusty walls—the village of Ojos Calientes, Mrs. Babb's Mexican neighbors. In back of the hotel I could see a dike which had apparently been bulldozed up along the river to prevent any more flood damage to the hotel. Close to the hotel was a large deserted greenhouse, no doubt constructed by H. L. Hunt, who had been interested in growing *Aloe vera* on a large scale.

I walked down and across the grounds to the dike, then walked along the top of it, looking over into the grove of trees on the other side of the river. From that vantage point, I spotted a rope bridge which had been constructed across the river. I tried my end of it; it was strong and the wooden steps seemed sound, so I walked across. The river was only a trickle underneath the bridge. Yet, walking across, each step seemed loaded with significance. The bridge on the other side led off into the grove of desert willows, and there was a well-worn path leading through the trees toward the village I had already spotted from a distance. Once at the grove, however, I thought better of going into the village by myself. A sense of my own isolation and complete vulnerability suddenly overwhelmed me, and I found myself almost running back across the bridge to the hotel's veranda, which had become in those minutes a symbol of life and civilization for me. For the next half an hour, I sat on the veranda trying to regain my nerve for the long trip back. Sitting there, I tried to imagine Mrs. Babb living for so many years by herself on this border in those expanses of white-crusted sand, the faint voices of the villagers which carried at times over the river, the cool winter air, and the mountains rushing up only yards away from the main gate.

There is a wildness in this part of Texas not found anywhere else. Driving back by myself along the river from the hot springs, following the dirt road that curves with the river bed, I continued to feel an acute separation between myself and all other human beings, which was both frightening and exciting at the same time. Mexico was always only a stone's throw away. There was nothing on my side of the river along the stretch except for the hotel at the springs I had left behind me and an occasional rough sign pointing off to the north: "Love Ranch" or "Private/No Trespassing." But on the other side of the river there were several clusters of roofs and adobe huts, little villages like Ojos Calientes with people whose ancestors no doubt had been familiar with this area hundreds of years ago. That is the civilization which is strongest here. On that side of the river there are many who believe that witches are in the area, and girls cry at night because the witches are supposed to come to beat them with chains. Spells are cast and countered by *brujas* known to every village. And, according to Mrs. Babb, the crows which roost in the mesquite along the river are believed by the villagers to belong to witches, or perhaps are the witches themselves transformed into birds. She told me that a reporter was sent one time to the village of Ojinaga, purportedly a center of witchcraft, but he never reported again to his magazine and was found months later dead in a cave. It was one thing to sit in Mrs. Babb's cozy Valentine living room listening to her recall these tidbits of border lore and quite another to remember her stories while driving home.

On my side of the river there was nothing to keep me company but the steep crags jutting up from the river plain bare and rocky because of the season. I traveled, as Mrs. Babb had instructed me, with a sleeping bag, a jug of water, and a box of canned goods. She said that it was crazy to start a trip in the desert without these items, and I am sure she was right. Something large and brown moved suddenly along a rock ledge above the car. I slowed down to see, thinking it might be a coyote or one of Wayne's panthers. But it lifted its head, and I saw that it was a wild burro, tawny brown with a white muzzle and dark rings around its eyes. By itself in the wilderness, it was a very beautiful animal and seemed to have little to do with the comic creature burdened with sticks or pots I had seen in the Juárez streets. He stared at me, refusing to budge, even when I stopped the car completely. In this country, he was clearly much more sure of himself than I was. In a minute he was joined by another, darker burro. They continued to stare at me implacably and remained in their position while I started up again and drove away slowly until a curve separated us and I was alone again.

I made the drive without incident, but it was a relief when the asphalt suddenly appeared and I was on the highway again, headed for El Paso. The occasional car that I passed on the highway seemed comforting and friendly. And I promised myself that, though I would very well like to visit the hot springs again, I would not go alone.

CHAPTER 9

Desert Years

Narrated by Jewel Babb

WHEN I LOST the hot springs, the only house I had to move back in was the tie house, or camp as hunters called it. It was no house and hardly a barn, it was so bad, and we hadn't been doing more with it for several years than storing beds and furniture in it. My son Dixie had built it in the forties, and since it was Mexican laborers who had built it, it was made by ear. When it rained, no way could the water be kept out. It was built in a hole scooped out of the side of the hill, so that way, about half of the house was setting underground, and a part above ground fronting a deep little canyon. Even with ditches dug and dirt thrown up around the back and sides of the structure, water still got into the house. Since it was made of railroad ties, it was very uneven. There were big cracks between the ties that let all the icy air in.[1]

When my son first made it, he put heavy tar paper all on the outside. But a man had been keeping cattle up there which had chewed off the tar paper covering it, exposing gaps between the ties sometimes half an inch wide. Agustín and I stuffed up the cracks with paper and pieces of plastic and tried to recover it as best we could.

Since it was handy for hunters, they would come and camp there in the old house. Of course, they'd be drinking and wanting to try out their guns. Trigger happy. So they would shoot holes through the top of the house. Bullets did not go through the ties so good, so they'd aim mostly at the top or roof.

It was a terrible place to move back to, and winter was near, and it was already getting cold. After living the months before in Arkansas visiting my daughter, Azalea, my eyes could hardly take the cold dry wind in this country, and my complexion suffered, too. Somehow I'd misplaced my cold cream. But I did have a can of fresh Crisco. So I used that, and it was good. But my eyes had to tough it out since I had no eye drops.

I'd brought my two German shepherds back from Arkansas with me, also my big feather quilts. Agustín put up an old iron wood heater. But we had no damper. So of course all the heat went up the stove pipes and did not even warm the old place up. And there was no wood. Just some sotol stumps down in the canyon. They were hard to carry up. I'd put them in the stove, and the sotol burned like paper. And some long posts someone had left there. I would nigger them in two[2] so I could get them inside the stove.

When Agustín helped me fix up all he could, he left me. And I was alone, just my two dogs and me. I had a few groceries and about ten gallons of water in glass jugs, as there was no water and no car to go bring water in. There was only an earthen tank that caught water when it rained for the animals—the horses, burros, cows, coyotes, and all the others that came by to drink. Bobcats, porcupines, and skunks. They all drank from this water. A few times I drank it myself. I'd strain it, then boil it and strain it again, then put a bucket full out in the sun and air, let it cool and use it. It was really pretty good. In the heat, I would put it in a deep container and wrap it up in rags to keep it cool. I only had a kerosene lamp, and sometimes, for days, no kerosene. That didn't bother me so much, because I usually went to bed at dark anyway. There were no pens for the animals that I was to have later. But there was an old open garage-like shed. The top of it was also shot full of bullet holes.

Since this old house was built up on a high hill, it was colder. High winds and rain were harder there, it seemed. The house was about two miles from Mexico and the Rio Grande. From one side and the front, you could look over into Mexico. Then north and back of the house, you could look down and across the famous Mayfield Canyon—famous, I'm told, for the ammonite fossils that are found there. Seems to me Mayfield was a mile deep. And it wasn't very far from my back door. There was only a rough trail going from the back of the house down into this canyon. Mexicans coming out of Mexico used this trail coming by burros or afoot from the Rio Grande. The trail was rough and dangerous.

Once in a while I went to different places to help take care of some sick people. And with part of the money I made, my daughter and son-in-law and I went down to a ranch near Presidio, Texas, where I bought an old nannie and six young kids. They were milk goats. I was really proud of them, and after that, I decided I'd just stay out there and try to make my living raising goats. I never did want to be a burden for my children or live with them and cause them trouble, like some mothers-in-law I'd seen. But, no, in the eight years I was there, I never did make real good, even when I raised several hundred. Varmints would catch them if the goats slept out in the mountains. Sometimes part of them would run off. And I'd never see them again. Rattlesnakes would bite and kill them, too, or leave them crippled. They would get bitten on the udders or legs. I'd put coal oil on the place, and in a few days yellow water would come out of the wound. Then maybe in a week or so they would be over it. Rattlesnakes were everywhere, even in the house I lived in.

And worst of all in this old country was the long, hard winter and spring. It would bring starvation, death, and sorrow. Death to the animals that were not fed. And sorrow to the ranchers that had to buy this high-priced feed.

When I got the seven goats, I had no pens, so I'd tie the old momma goat close to the house, and the younger ones would stay close to her and not run off. Later on, my son bought five more. A rancher also brought a few more. Then I had seventeen. And no pens, or shelter for them. One day, my daughter came, and the two of us built a small pen. A man from Mexico came over and built a shed for shelter, since it was wintertime. My son Wayne went to Dell City and bought a load of milo maize, heads and all. So I just kept these goats in the pen and fed them all winter and spring. Carried water from the tank for them (a goat doesn't drink too much water) or I melted the snow. And they'd drink that water.

During all this time, I had no car and no way of going anywhere. I just depended on three people to bring in the things I needed—groceries, mail, and water. And I'll always be thankful to my son Wayne, Agustín, and a woman friend, Mrs. Susie Fields of Oklahoma City. I could never have stayed there had they not helped me. Of course, my neighbors from Mexico would come and help me now and then, too. They were good neighbors. But they lived a long ways off.

I did not have enough bedding. So my friend from Oklahoma City would come with a pick-up load of clothes that could be made into quilts, and some old dresses that could be worn around the house. And also feather beds—big ones. I would sleep on them and cover with heavy feather quilts, and I'd be warm. Even though the gallons of water would freeze and break at night at the foot of my bed. I would heat up rocks, too, and put my feet on them to keep warm. The cold of a morning was terrible. Then when summer did come, I only had an arbor frame with only a little cover left on top of it for shade. During the day it would be hot, and I was glad for a little shade. I think the weather is still pretty much the same, but over the years I have gotten used to it.

There were no locks at any time on my doors, and when summer came, I moved my bed outside and slept out of the house. Each night as I lay in bed, I could hear the coyotes calling close by. Then a fox now and then. Also the night birds singing. The old hoot owl would tune in now and then with the other birds. Then there was the tiny elf owl. I loved its song best of all, and each springtime I looked forward to their coming. By the seventeenth of each March they were there and always used the same old posts or tree trunks they'd used for years. I'd finally go to sleep hearing all these wonderful sounds.

I'd always get up early in the morning to do what I had to for the day. One morning, though, I was awakened just at daylight. I was sleeping outside, and somewhere I heard a rattlesnake buzzing. I could tell it was mad by the way it rattled. So I raised my head and looked all around. Someone had brought two hens several days before, and one of them was black. And this old black hen was jumping up and trying to get something off the old screen door. A big rattler had been asleep right inside of the door in the house. The hen had woke the snake up, and it was mad. But it couldn't get to the hen to bite her. The snake was rattling extra loud. I got up when I saw where the snake was, found a short pole, and run the old hen away. Then I stood back away from the screen door, opening it up a tiny bit at a time until I could see this big snake all coiled there waiting to bite me if I were to step inside. Then I killed it with the pole, and it was a big one. I was very thankful to that old hen for saving me.

Another time I'd gone to town for the night, and Wayne was staying at the tie camp alone. He said he'd gone to bed, and the night was very dark, when one of the shepherds began to bark. He called to her and tried to stop her from barking. But she kept on. Finally, he thought he'd better go see what she was barking at. So he got out of bed and went outside barefooted. She was still barking, and he was looking toward the mountain there close by, thinking she was barking at a coyote there. But, no. When he was nearly to the dog, he saw she was barking at something nearly at his foot. Then he looked down, too. Another step and he would have stepped on a big rattlesnake.

That same summer, I needed to drive my goats to the dirt tank a half-mile away. Since they were thirsty, I had no trouble taking them to the water. But I was close behind them when they got to the tank and was drinking. I started down the big tank dump. Close to the water I slipped and fell down. When I looked down, I saw a horse had left its track there in the mud about three inches deep. And there, coiled up in the track, was a rattlesnake. He was asleep in the warm sun. It did not even raise its head up or rattle. When I could get up and away from it, I got a stick and killed it. That was the first time in my life I'd ever seen a snake act like that. But I was always on the lookout for snakes because they were everywhere. I'd get up early in the morning in the summertime and go outside. I always found one to kill.

When I was out of feed for my goats, each day I'd start out with them. I'd herd them up to eight miles from the ranch, just going here and there up on the high mountains, then down in the little valleys. Any place where the goats could find something to eat, as when we had a dry spell there was no vegetation. I always carried a little bottle of water. And sometimes the days were so hot, I put a wet towel on top of my head under my head scarf. Each summer I had to wear towels like this, even after Wayne built a porch on this old house. Setting on the porch sometimes was like setting in an oven.

Several times while herding the goats, I'd set on a high point of a mountain, and I'd see six or eight deer, young ones and their mommas, grazing along with the goats. I'd watch and see if the deer and goats fought. But, no, they were friendly. And each was busy eating. The deer would not run off until I walked down close to them. Sometimes they came right on home with the goats. Black-tailed deer. And I could raise them right with the goats. I never had any goats stolen. And I didn't brand them either. I had one of my boys come out there one time, and no brand, no gun, no rope. And he says, "My mother thinks nobody else has any goats. She doesn't have a brand on them." But I don't like branding. I don't believe in it unless you have to. I used to have to do it when I was married and living on the ranch, but I never liked to. Cut the ears off, that's awful. But that's the way the ranchers made their mark. Cut off one ear, cut a big slice out of the other. But my own goats were every color you can imagine, and they didn't have a mark on them. I never knew sometimes how many I had, but I think I got up to 350 at one time.

In those days, Indians from Mexico would come across hunting medicine plants and, above all, the cactus peyote.[3] Six or seven of these men would walk up to the house wanting something to eat or water. The Indians were great beggars and always wanted you to give them anything that they could carry off. Sometimes they'd show me the different medicine plants they'd gathered and what each plant was for in curing. I learned lots from them and also from the old men and women that were my neighbors living in Mexico that came to see me at different times. One bunch of Indians came to see me from Oklahoma. They were looking for the cactus peyote. And as we talked, one said, "If you have faith, an ordinary rock could cure you."

Before I was at the tie camp, I was living at Indian Hot Springs. But I knew I was going to have to leave. And I was scared. I had learned in the eight years that I was there how to heal with the water, mosses, and mud. And in all the eight years there, I had needed no doctor or medicine. So I thought, when I leave this place, what will I do? No money for doctors nor hospitals. So one day a man came to the springs. He was helping the sick by massaging the pressure points in the feet and the points that are all over the body. He called it zone therapy. He was working with the people across in Mexico, and just anybody that would let him massage their feet. After seeing this way of healing, I knew I had to learn that way of curing the sick, my family, myself, and friends. He stayed at the springs nearly two weeks. He showed me all the points in the feet and how to massage them. I knew then that this way of massaging could be used when I could no longer use the mineral waters and the muds and mosses. He also sent me a book of instruction on zone therapy. I'd had a good start, and everything was easy for me. Also, I had experience as I went along, too. Through all these years, before and after living at the tie house, I kept studying. And then I was learning to heal with my mind. Even at a distance.

So. I would tell these Indian doctors and old men from Mexico, herbs and such is good. But you have to buy or gather them. Sometimes maybe you can't get the healing plants that you want. But the hands and mind you have right with you at all times. Of course, it's good to know about the medicine plants. There were so many good plants around the place, and I've always used them. But in these years, I've found my hands are better. These Indian men were very smart in their way of healing with plants, and they went all through the border country gathering the plants on both sides of the Rio Grande. But some of the best plants are starting to disappear.

And people would still come to the tie camp to see me. Even with everything run down and hard to get to. One man came driving up with his wife in a station wagon. He had an obstruction and had been told he should go to a surgeon. Well, his wife was snotty about this dirty house and this dirty old woman. She looked out into the sky while her husband talked to me. I looked just awful. My hem shredded up from the goats. So I told them to wait in the car until I swept the floor. Then they came on in. And the obstruction was released in just five seconds with stomach massage. After that, his wife acted like she was my best friend.

But while living at the tie camp, I was in danger all the time, day and night, especially from the rattlesnakes. I kept on doing the things I wanted to do, though—herd my goats of a morning, come into the house about one or two o'clock in the evening,[4] pen the goats, eat a little, then for two or three hours get my books and lessons and study. Then when it was later and cooler in the evening, go out with my goats again. I was never too lonesome, because I was busy all times. And in a way, I was happy. I was closer to God out there in the wilderness. I could understand him better. I know that the Bible is the foundation of all knowledge, but I've studied it on my own. If you go to church, you'll just hear it how they tell it. But if you sit on a hill for fifteen years with your animals and no one else, you learn a lot. It comes to you. David did it with his sheep.[5] And, above all, I know that God takened care of me all these years. And even though I fell and sometimes hurt myself real bad, I healed real quick and was able to go on with my work. Through all the twenty years I've been living in the desert, I feel like I've helped many people that would come to me sick, and I've helped myself, too. I've had heart trouble many years, but I know how to treat it.

While I was herding my goats out in the hills, I did lots of exploring. There were little limestone caves that I'd look into. Caves that had been used by the Indians a long time ago. Some were pretty big and others were smaller. There were big caves in the bluffs that overlooked Mayfield Canyon. But I was afraid of them, as these rocks were rotten and crumbled easily. After a rain or real cold spell, some of the top rocks of these high places would break loose and slide down the mountainside. One was close to my house, a big formation of rocks that stood on a high point. One evening, I looked at this place. And next morning when I looked again, it was gone, rocks and all, everything slid down the mountainside. So this part of the country, I soon learned, was dangerous. And I did not go over or into this part often. And wherever I went with the goats, I always was watching for the herbs the Indians tell me about. Some of these plants only grow in the high places. Others in the little valleys. Still other plants are only found in crevices of rocks, under the shrubbery, or sheltered places.

Soon I had a bunch of baby kids. Also a litter of snow-white German shepherd puppies. Soon as all were old enough to follow me with the goats, they would run along beside me, getting into the thorns and barking. The baby kids also found out about the cactus and thorns. But they would all tire out soon and have to rest in the shade. I'd find a dagger plant and set down in its shade. Right quick the baby kids came and lay down close to me as they could get, ten or twelve of the little animals. Then the white baby dogs wanted to rest and get as close to me as possible. But no way, as the baby goats were all around me. So all the puppies could do was to climb up on the baby kids and go to sleep there. But we could never rest too long, as the grown goats would wander off to eat, and we would have to get up and follow them. All this time we were resting, the puppies' momma and papa were running rabbits and other varmints around the goats. But the goats did not mind. They were used to all this barking and running through them. Sometimes I had to step up a rock ledge two feet or more high. The babies (pups and kids) could not jump up on top or get over this ledge of rock. Then I'd have to lift each one up on top so that we might go on after the herd. It was a very pretty sight seeing all these young animals running along after the goats. Snow-white puppies, black, brown, white, or spotted baby goats. All of them close together.

My white German shepherd was a great watchdog. She was good to watch the goats in the daytime. But in the night she was a killer and might even kill the goats. She only loved two things in the world, and one was Wayne. Her and him would run and play around the house for hours. Then she loved me. And every other thing, she thought should die or be killed. My daughter brought her big German shepherd out with eight puppies and left them with me for a few months with my white dog and her pups, along with two of my other white dogs. I had seventeen German shepherds then. When a car drove up to my place, no one got out. They'd even roll their window glass up. So many big fierce-looking dogs. As the baby pups got older, there was just one in all the bunch I wanted. She was black, brown, and gray, a beautiful animal. She was not friendly with no one but me. I named her Tiger-Bell. She was always with the goats and me and was good with them. She learned to go around them and bring them back or drive them into the pens. Everything was fine until the baby kids began coming. Then Tiger-Bell decided they'd all better be killed, and she'd kill them, too. No matter what kind of beating I'd give her. So finally I had to tie Tiger-Bell up.

Mexican officers came to the tie house when they made a trip to the Indian Hot Springs and would come in and talk a while. They always admired and tried to talk to Tiger-Bell. In time, they made friends with her. Then later on she liked the Mexican officers as long as they wore the pretty caps that officers wore on their heads and as long as they had their uniforms on. If not, she'd bite them, or try to. I knew I would have to give her away, as she would not stop killing the baby kids. So one officer, especially, wanted her. One day he came by, and I gave him Tiger-Bell. Afterward, he said she made a wonderful watchdog at his home in Ojinaga, Mexico, and no one but an officer could come in his yard. But he sure better have his cap on.

At first, the Mexicans came out of Mexico two or three at a time looking for work. They had only tortillas and a little tobacco with them. And they were always hungry and thirsty. But as the years passed, more and more came across. One morning I got up early and walked out to the goat pen. Looking across a small deep canyon, I counted twelve Mexican men just setting over there watching me. About this time the dogs barked in front of the house. So I turned and walked back to the front. And there were seven more Mexicans standing looking at me from a small hill. But they never came to the house that time. Just went on.

Another time, one morning early, the dogs were tied but they were barking. And I went to look outside. There were ten Mexican men standing there. They didn't look like the Mexicans I'd see most every day coming by. They were mean looking and had yellow complexions. One of them said real quick, "We want you to take us to the nearest town now."

By then I had an old car. But I said, "I can't. My car has no gasoline in the tank, and the nearest town is twenty-eight miles away. I'll have to wait until someone brings me some gasoline."

One of the men turned to another and said, "Go check the gas tank."

And he did. And saw there was no gas. Then I told them, "If I did try to take you all to town, officers would stop us, and you would be caught."

But they weren't scared in the least. About this time, they looked over on the road and saw a car coming a long way off, and they thought if they'd go down the road toward this car, they might get a ride. So they all hurried off.

Each day seemed that more and more passed by, until they were coming by in bunches of eighteen and twenty. Then I began to see someone had planned all this, as these men were well equipped. They had sardines, coffee, tobacco, and tortillas. Good canned food. Then as I began to see more of these strange people creeping, walking, and running into our way of life, hurrying to get into their own place and be ready for the terrible chaos that we all know is coming.[6] I could see that all of this just didn't happen. It had been well planned, and we were being silently invaded. And most people didn't know it. This was still happening when I left there, but I had gotten used to all the dangers. I never kept a gun either. I can shoot a gun, but I don't believe in them. A Ranger asked me once if I had a gun, and I said, "No, what would I want with a gun?" He said somebody might come and kill me. I said, "No, if I had a gun and killed somebody, then the government would kill me!" So he didn't say no more.

One morning I walked out with my goats. I was still close to the house when I looked up, and there was a bright object about as big as a football, lavender, yellow, orange, red, and green, bright as could be. And it was falling to the ground. It wasn't falling straight down, but rather it was slanted and falling fast. When it did hit the ground, there was, it seemed, just a puff. And then it was gone, leaving no trace. I know, because I went and looked. Just nothing where some sign should have been.

A few nights later, I was alone and it was nearly daylight. I was awake laying on my right side just thinking. When all of a sudden, something got hold of my upper left arm and side, tighter, tighter, and in my mind I knew I couldn't get loose from whatever held me. I didn't seem to be scared. I just lay there thinking, how am I ever going to get loose from this thing. By this time, I was held so tight against the bed I could not move. So I just lay there. After more time had passed, the hold on my arm began to loosen until it had gone. There was no one in the house but myself. *That* I know for sure.

Then the next night, must have been toward morning, too, something woke me, and I opened my eyes. And the whole house, even outside, was bright as day. I looked around the room and could see every little thing. The light stayed for a while, then began to fade away. And there was no one on the place but me. The dogs did not even bark. Whatever these things were, I felt no different in the days afterward. Everything went on as usual.

Another time, I was up early in the morning and decided I'd go out in the goat pen and see if the goats were all right. As I passed by the old barn, there stood a big fat man, and what I could see of the poorest, tiredest, oldest horse I've ever seen. The horse looked like some kind of over-sized hat rack. There was an old, old saddle on him. There were old ragged blankets and quilts just thrown across the saddle, hanging down on either side of the horse. Little white sacks of tortillas and cakes tied and hanging down on the saddle. Coffee pot tied on another part of the saddle. Frying pans and pots tied here and there. A rope coiled and laid across the old horn of the saddle, a coat tied in another place, and a water jug. I could hardly believe my eyes, so many things on this poor old horse. Then I looked at the big fat man, and he was laughing. After talking a while with him, he asked if he couldn't camp there close by and help me out with my work. So I told him he could. He stayed and was a good worker and a good man.

One day, he was gone with the goats and was to stop and work on a barbed-wire fence. He left and was gone until mid-evening. When I looked and saw him coming in, I was surprised, as it was too early for him to come back. But I thought there must be a reason. So I just forgot about him and kept on thinking and looking out over the hills. When he rode up to the door, he got off and tied up his horse. He opened the old door and stepped in. Then I saw, from his knee down, that blood was running like water down and off his pant leg, and his shoe was full of blood. Only thing he said was, a wire cut him. Right quick, I made him set down and elevate his foot and leg. Then I grabbed a whole gallon of kerosene oil that Agustín had brought out the day before. And since I didn't take time to see where the wound was, I poured the oil all over his leg. I kept this up every so often, and finally there was no more blood. After I knew the blood had stopped, I got the scissors and cut away the pants to where I could see the wound. I cleaned the blood off, and all I could see was a small hole on top of the vein in his leg. Next morning he was able to walk about two miles following after his poor horse. Of course, there are many ways to stop blood. Old timers use this verse in the Bible—Ezekiel 16:6—and they do it for animals, too. But I've never used it myself.[7]

A good many days after that, one evening he came to the back door. His throat all swelled up after being out in a freezing wind all day. It was so bad he could hardly talk. Said it hurt him too much. I said, "Go set down across the porch from me." He did. I stood looking at his throat. After a few seconds, the swelling started going away. A few more minutes, and all the swelling was gone. And he got up and went on to his camp. Next day, it was colder. I told him to wrap his throat up good before getting out in this cold weather. He said, "I'm not afraid. If I get sick, you can cure me."

One summer, Wayne wanted to get some hounds to run the mountain lions. Their hides and bounty was good. So he was in hopes of catching a few. He began to look around for hounds. But no one had the kind of dogs he wanted. So one day as he was reading a magazine, he saw an advertisement where a man had the very dogs he wanted in Arkansas. So he sat down and answered the advertisement. In a few days, the man from Arkansas wrote and said he had three—fine big game dogs already trained—and especially they were trained not to run rabbits.

So Wayne sent the money after the dogs. In a week or so, the dogs were at the depot. Wayne tied them up and fed them for over a week to be sure they wouldn't run off, and if they did, they would know where to come back to. After enough time had passed, he turned them loose so they might get a little exercise. They were glad to get loose and run around the house a little. One got away from the house, and a big fat jackrabbit jumped up in front of the hound. You never saw such a race. Finally, all the three were running and barking after the jackrabbit. All the time Wayne was calling them to stop. No, sir. None paid any attention. Just kept on going. Old Arkansas Annie, the momma dog's name, finally got in the lead. Soon all was out of hearing.

Wayne got his horse to go see if he could find the dogs. But, no. He could find no trace of them. Finally, he came back and said, "I can't find or hear them. But they will come back tonight." But we never saw those dogs again. Wayne rode and hunted them for days. But they had just disappeared. Wayne said, "I guess a truck or car picked them up." About four months later, a Mexican was digging out a shallow well down in a big canyon, and there was the dogs. They had drowned in this well, I guess, still trying to follow that rabbit. Some dogs. But that was how that country was. Human or animal both would die there if they didn't know their own way around it.

Last year my old herder came in one evening. He always started talking real loud when he'd found something. He said, "Come here. I found an Indian head."

He was swinging a skull. He had the man's belt and his head. He said he saw the goats run and start chewing on bones and found a skeleton. So I went and told the officers. And the sheriff, a deputy, immigration, and all came out to the place. So my herder is a wetback, but he wasn't scared. He takened them. It was so steep they couldn't stand up straight at the spot. There was a little sheepdog, and he started digging, too. They said it was a boy about fourteen years old. There was one little piece of Levis, and they put all his bones in a sack and brought it back to the tie house.

Sometimes I would just stand outside my cabin and look across all those hills, over to the faraway blue mountains of Mexico and across the great valley of greasewood all the same color of green stretching out for miles. And I would wonder about my life being tied up in this desert. And I would think about death, that is always just a breath away. Then I would turn around, and there would be the sunset. Beautiful beyond description. And I think there will be a time I can step right off my hill and walk right up through it. And maybe I will just go away that way.

CHAPTER 10

Afterword

TO ISOLATE Mrs. Babb's role as a faith healer is a distortion not only of the way she perceives herself but also of the way in which she is perceived by the outside observer, who in this case was myself. To Mrs. Babb, her ability to heal is seen as a gift, just as is the ability to raise *Aloe vera* and grandchildren. To me, she is primarily a strong, yet compassionate, woman, able to be at home in a desert environment that most of us would consider at best unfriendly, at worst unlivable. In recounting her story, she gave at least as much emphasis to her trials and tribulations as a young bride and mother as to the manifestations of healing abilities and spirit helpers. The larger story is the record of how one woman came to maturity, weathered adverse circumstances, both environmental and human, and came out all the stronger for it; the ability to "heal with the mind" is only a small part of the story. Even in her own recounting, I am afraid that my confessed interest in her ability to heal led her into certain emphases on the material that she might not have chosen herself. Davidson and Day, in eliciting the personal history of another healer, Nora Cabral, pointed out that autobiographical materials were selectively chosen by the healer in terms of her present role.[1] Yet they do not acknowledge enough, I think, the fact that the present had been made in part by themselves, coming to the healer with pad and pencil in hand. Carlos Castañeda acknowledges this problem of the researcher in his third book, *Journey to Ixtlan*, when he realizes that his first book was a complete distortion because of his own preoccupation with a thesis having to do with hallucinogenic drugs. I have this kind of worry myself. The conversations I had with Mrs. Babb which were not recorded were much more extensive than the ones which were. The information she gave me on other facets of her life was at least as extensive as the information she gave me on healing. She herself implicitly acknowledged this imbalance recently by beginning a manuscript devoted to her goats—their stories, their foibles, their diseases and how to deal with them—because, to her, goats are at least as large in her life as is faith healing.

However, Mrs. Babb's role as faith healer held a great degree of interest for me, and for that reason I urged her on in that area while I might not have urged her in others. Further, I included the word *healing* in the title of our book rather than *mother* or *goatherder* (although these well could be parallel stories stemming from the same present, given a different emphasis from a different guide than myself).

But it seemed to me that Mrs. Babb's role as faith healer was of interest to the study of folk medicine in general, as an example of the survival and revitalization of a tradition encouraged by the border culture of which Mrs. Babb is a part. Whereas several writers on the subject of folk medicine have emphasized the homogeneity of the healers and their communities, it seemed to me that Mrs. Babb in many respects was apart from the Anglo ranching community; at the same time, she saw herself as bringing together otherwise disparate communities—Anglo with Mexican, poor with rich, Negro with white. This sense of herself as cultural medium was quite evident, for instance, in her story of the hot springs, a place where Mexicans, Negroes, Creoles, and Cajuns came together, many times speaking different languages, in order to be healed. What factors, then, were present in Mrs. Babb's particular brand of folk medicine which allowed her to serve as such a cultural bridge? Or were those factors inherent to a certain extent in her location in a border area itself? In one study of *curanderismo*, the researcher James Sherman states that "in order for the folk healer or the medical practitioner to be effective, his treatment modality must be in line with the belief system within which he practices and must therefore fulfill the expectations of the patient."[2] If this is true, then Mrs. Babb's growing popularity with members of disparate ethnic backgrounds must be built on a set of qualifications equally appealing to segments of both communities. At the same time, in her particular location, due to the fact of isolation where human beings must depend upon each other regardless of racial background, a border culture might be emerging which itself honored certain values of both ethnic backgrounds, forming a new matrix for folk medicine in which Mrs. Babb participated.

The Anglo folk healing tradition of Mrs. Babb's Appalachian roots and Protestant origins has not been studied and analyzed as definitively as have the folk healing traditions of other cultures. This has not been the fault so much of folklorists and researchers as it is a symptom of the disrepute and lack of respect generally accorded in our culture to the tradition itself. This has been particularly true of those aspects of folk healing associated with religious or psychic principles, many of which are rooted in antiquity and were originally channeled into Christianity. In one history of the Anglo tradition, Don Yoder has traced the Anglo problems in accepting those aspects of folk medicine to the Protestant Reformation.[3] Prior to that time, the primitive drive to connect faith and healing had been sanctioned by the church. Within the growing cult of saints, particular saints had been chosen as healing agents who interceded with God on behalf of the patient and who, many times, were responsible for miraculous cures. Because the association of healing with saints had become so prevalent, when the Protestants took belief in saints away from the church doctrine, they essentially drove the folk healing associated with them underground, and thereafter only formal prayers for the sick were permitted within the church structure. In Catholic cultures, folk healing has continued to be an integral part of the church and community structure, whereas in Protestant communities folk healing has been relegated to certain lay practitioners who, at best, have been regarded with a certain amount of suspicion and, at worst, have been persecuted for their healing talents. A case in point was a woman named Margaret Jones who, in 1648, was hanged in Charlestown, Massachusetts—the fact that she could effect cures with herbs was enough evidence to prove her a witch.[4]

More recently, faith healing has gradually emerged again in this country and in this century and has become a part of some church rituals, including Christian Science and the Pentecostal sects. In the process, however, the most widely recognized faith healer model has been divested of all of its medical trappings except the purely religious. No diagnoses or prescriptions are made, and there is no pretense of knowledge of the physical body. Medicine is left up to the physician; the faith healer handles only that portion of the patient which belongs to God, which, presumably, is the spirit only. Even individual faith healers outside a particular church structure adhere to this "separation of church and state." When setting up business, they tend to follow the church-minister-congregation pattern rather than a healer-patient tradition. The less prosperous healers will reserve a room in their homes for services, many times equipping the room with a pulpit and altar rail which separates the minister from his or her following. The same arrangement will be essentially followed for the more popular healers, who might use a large tent and tour the country. The healing sessions are generally preceded by singing and preaching in order to "call down" the Holy Spirit, which will effect whatever cures are asked for. One example of this type of faith healer is the well-known Katherine Kuhlman. Another, more local, example is the "Seer of Corsicana," Annie Buchanan, who operates a sanctuary out of her own house and is known for her passionate preaching and singing.[5] The emphasis in such sessions is as much on the exhortation to "be saved" as it is to "be healed," in Protestant fashion. Even those sects, however, which approve of faith healing per se view the independent faith healer with a suspect eye because of the lack of church affiliation. According to Pentecostal doctrine, the gifted individual (i.e., the one whose faith is strong enough to effect healing) is a prime target for the devil and needs the protection of the larger church body within which to practice the gift. It would be wrong, therefore, to say that faith healers who utilize the model of church-minister-congregation in their healing ceremonies have obtained a role within the healing structure of a particular community. In fact, they are outside the structure so long as they are not members of a particular church, and approval is withheld from the very structure which gave them the role model to follow.

The separation of the physical and spiritual aspects of healing in the Anglo healing tradition has also been encouraged by the professional medical institutions, which have waged a powerful and consistent battle, both legal and propagandistic, against all forms of "quackery," which has included folk medicine and any form of faith healing which would presume to treat the body outside the confines of religion.[6] As a result of this powerful combination of censure from both church and medical institutions, the Anglo community has provided little encouragement to its folk healers.

As a result, Anglo settlers were slower and less prone to learn about North American native herbs and Indian medical practices than were black slaves and Spanish settlers. It was not until the 1800s that records began to be printed in English of Indian root doctors, many times by white men who would apprentice themselves to the medicine men and write down their stories. The 1800s also saw the rise of several medical movements, such as hydropathy and homeopathy, both attempts to give average people a set of medical rudiments whereby they could take charge of their own well-being, diagnosing and administering cures to themselves, without having to rely upon the medical professional. Such movements became popular in a frontier country where the population continued to move away from urban centers into areas where little or no professional medical care was available. These systems relied primarily on herbs, fresh air, sunshine, exercise, proper diet (often vegetarian), and water treatments. By the early nineteen hundreds, however, the professional medical institution had again gained control of medicine in this country, making it illegal to practice medicine without a license, including midwifery in many states. Thus, folk healing, if it was practiced at all, could not be practiced for money and therefore was generally restricted to home remedies administered within the confines of the household, either in not-so-serious cases of illness, when professional medical care was deemed unnecessary, or in cases of poverty, when the financial means were not available to obtain professional medical care, or in cases of geographical isolation, when professional medical care was too far away to do any good.

Yet, the full-time Anglo folk healer, throughout the centuries of both church and professional medical persecution, continued to exist, particularly in rural and insulated communities. More often than not, they had an intimate knowledge of the natural elements of their surroundings which could be used for healing—the plants, water, minerals, and fresh air—and were known variously as an "herb-doctor," a "witch-doctor," or a "pow-wower." A profile of such healers has been furnished by Don Yoder, who describes the "power doctor" in the Ozarks as one who, in addition to herbs, uses charms, amulets, and physical manipulation; who heals by ritual and by the spoken word; and who sees himself as a channel of healing power from a divine source. Although Yoder's "power doctor" is more generally male than female, the "wise-woman" and "granny-wife" are his female counterparts and are still mentioned by Ozark informants.

The full-time healer, however, has been difficult to interview. Probably, there are very few of them left; in addition, Yoder has called this kind of healer a person apart because even in rural communities the folk healer role is not considered entirely respectable. The healer therefore tends to live alone and remain inaccessible. By far the commonest healers that folklorists have interviewed have not been full-time healers such as this, but rather part-time specialists in one of three traditional areas: "talking out fire," "healing 'thrash,'" and "stopping blood." Generally, a secret verse or charm is murmured by the healers while they perform certain gestures with their hands or use their breath to blow into the affected area. However,

Eliot Wigginton, who publishes the *Foxfire* books and has done research in this area, has found widespread disagreement among the healers themselves on practically all aspects of the healing tradition, including the number of individuals they could teach, what sex the students should be, the physical motions employed during healing, and the number of times "secret verses" should be repeated, if verses were used at all.[7] This disagreement would indicate that much of the tradition has been fragmented and partially forgotten. When called upon, Wigginton's informants generally worked with neighbors and neighbors' children as a gesture of friendship rather than seeing themselves as primarily healers, and they accepted no money for their services. In addition, many of them only practiced one of the traditional specialties, rarely all three, and none of them seemed to be thought of as a general practitioner of folk medicine, equipped to diagnose and treat a variety of illnesses.

The only other type of folk healer that has continued to be active has been the granny-midwife of the rural and mountainous areas whose primary business is to "catch babies." But, as with other forms of folk healing, her practices have been discouraged by the professional medical associations, and midwifery has been outlawed completely in several states and gradually phased out of others, as in Arkansas, where midwifery licenses can no longer be renewed.

It is little wonder, then, that studies of Anglo folk medicine have tended to restrict themselves to compilations of various home remedies, sayings, and superstitions, fragments of traditional medical systems which have come down to the various informants within the family or have been learned helter-skelter from various neighbors. Many of these remedies involve the use of herbs, water, and various household stock supplies. However, as the population moved into areas of relatively new settlement, much of the herbal lore was forgotten or the plants became unavailable. In Texas, for instance, Anglo remedies of record generally rely more on household stock, such as lard, kerosene, bacon rind, and soda. In addition, various magico-religious elements are sprinkled throughout these remedies, usually in the form of charms and certain Bible verses to be used in specific cases of illness. But, generally, in these listings, it is difficult to determine if the practice cited by the informant is in active use or if it is considered hearsay or "superstition" by the informant and in fact is not used by that informant for medicinal purposes.

This, then, is the Anglo healing tradition from which Mrs. Babb's family came. Her family, as had other Anglo families that made the long trip from Tennessee into Texas, no doubt brought a number of home remedies with them and a certain knowledge of herbs and patent remedies. Jewel Babb recalls her grandmother, part-Indian Lucindy Belle Starr Wilson, as one who enjoyed taking care of sick people, administering footbaths, and giving certain herbal remedies. But there is no indication that her healing role extended beyond the limits of her own family or in any way into the magico-religious fields of folk healing dealing with divine powers.

However, as a child, Jewel Babb was taught something of plants and gained a genuine appreciation of the outdoors. She crisscrossed the West Texas plains with her family in a wagon, sleeping more in tents than in houses, until she was school age and her parents began thinking of a more permanent life for their children. Although she was very young when they moved to Del Rio, she still remembers the early wagon days as an idyllic time in her life. She recalls that time as one when she was close to the land, learning the habits of the animals and the secret places where wild plums and berries grew.

For the rest of her childhood, she was primarily a city girl, growing up in Del Rio and going to school. Here there was no real need for home medication, as modern medical facilities were available (which she would take advantage of later when she was delivering her children). But her love of the outdoors was firmly ingrained. As she says, "If you're loose all the time, you know, and have freedom, then you don't want to be penned up."

It is little wonder, then, that when she married Walter Babb, she refused to stay at home, insisting instead on riding the range with him and the other cowboys. When she was writing about this time of her life, Mrs. Babb told me it was a "study in pure ignorance. Not many people want to publish their mistakes. At first I didn't either. But got to thinking about it. And it all was laughable when I looked back over the years of long ago. So I put it down." But what she lacked in know-how, she made up in determination and independence, unwilling to ever take the more subservient, traditional woman's role. In a part of the country where the women who have successfully adapted have had to be stronger than their more urbanized sisters, Mrs. Babb learned to be even more independent than most. The model provided by her mother-in-law was apparently a good one for her, too, as the older woman comes across in these accounts as wise in the ways of ranching and capable of hunting and trapping her own food and slaughtering her own cattle, in addition to maintaining a household for the Babb men who were known in that part of the country for a certain wild streak.

It was probably at this point that Jewel Babb first came into contact with *curanderismo*, the rich folk healing tradition prevalent in the border country. The influence of this tradition on Anglo ranch hands on the various ranches and farms in Texas where they find themselves working side by side with Mexican hands has been well documented in one survey of Texas folk remedies collected by folklorist Frost Woodhull. In his extensive collection, certain phrases tend to repeat themselves: "I have frequently seen Mexicans . . . ,"[8] "One of the Mexicans on the ranch told me . . . ,"[9] "[a plant] is said to be much used in Mexico . . . ,"[10] ". . . *remedio* is used by some white men."[11] Other examples of cross-cultural influence are even more apparent in this collection when, for instance, advice is given to hang a picture of the Virgin Mary on a mesquite tree for a drought remedy or, in case of bed-wetting, to feed the patient the hind legs of a crisply fried rat. As Woodhull says of his findings, Texas pioneers generally believed in "agencies . . . tangible and visible, but semi-occasionally, and principally along the Rio Grande, reasons are not so readily apparent."[12] The difference between traditional Anglo home remedies in Texas and Mexican remedies, according to Woodhull, is the difference between "abrupt simplicity and Latin finesse."[13]

Unlike Anglo folk medicine, Mexican folk medicine has continued to receive widespread encouragement from the Mexican community and has resisted the efforts of the modern medical institution to discredit it. This is particularly true at the rural village level of the border area where Mrs. Babb is located, but the folk medicine has also proved surprisingly resilient even in urban areas, such as San Antonio, where a number of *curanderos*, or folk healers, are easily found. Some writers have attempted to explain the resistance of lower-class Mexican Americans to modern medicine in terms of its preservational function of a traditional life-style. Many of the diseases treated by *curanderos*, for instance, are traditional folk diseases, such as *susto*, *empacho*, and *mal de ojo*,[14] which the modern physician refuses to recognize on the basis of physical origin. According to one anthropologist, these traditional diseases tend to support a traditional way of life and require a traditional mode of treatment.[15] It would be erroneous, however, to see *curanderismo* as a function primarily of folk disease. A San Antonio study of *curanderos* found that the Mexican American community considered the folk healer to be very much the equivalent of the general practitioner, most commonly asked to cure headaches, anxiety, irritability, nervousness, depression, gastrointestinal problems, folk illnesses, hypertension, diabetes, renal problems, back pain, sexual problems, nonspecific pain, and individual or marital conflict.[16] According to researchers, the tendency among many Mexican Americans in need of medical care, particularly at the village level, is to first seek help at the *curandero* level and to work from the most accessible healer to the more well known, seeking out the modern medical physician only as a last resort. Such behavior seems to be the opposite of that of an Anglo in need of medical assistance, who has been conditioned to seek the help of physicians first and only as a last resort, if ever, to seek the help of a folk healer.

In the isolation of the West Texas desert, however, such niceties become a quibble, as many times the *curandero* is the only available medical practitioner around. According to a Texas Medical Association survey in 1973, there were still twenty-three counties in Texas without doctors,[17] the majority of them in West Texas and the Panhandle. Only five of the twenty-three counties had a population of three or more persons per square mile. Indian Hot Springs is located in the largest of these counties, Hudspeth, which contains 4,554 square miles and as of 1975 an estimated population of 2,968, or about half a person per square mile.[18] In these areas, the closest doctor might be more than a hundred miles away, the nearest hospital as far as three hundred miles distant. And the dangers inherent in the region are many, including not only the wide range of disease and illness found in more populous areas but also rattlesnake bites and the variety of wounds possible from active, outdoor life in rugged terrain. As Mrs. Babb told it, ". . . you had to be a doctor and you had to be a nurse if you was going to take care of a young baby a 100, 150 miles from a town."

But there is little indication that Mrs. Babb paid much attention to the *curanderismo* tradition as a young woman. Other than demonstrating an independent streak and a love of the country, she seemed to be cut from the same mold as many other ranching wives. If she learned anything of the *curanderismo* tradition, she probably learned it second-hand through her mother-in-law, as her own knowledge of Spanish was limited. It was not until she and her family moved from the Langtry, Texas, area to Sierra Blanca that her interest in healing grew beyond the simple techniques she had been using in lieu of modern medical care when the necessity arose.

Undoubtedly, the move to the hot springs was the major turning point in Mrs. Babb's life. For one thing, it opened up a complete field of knowledge which she had not been aware of before. As she says, ". . . we was just ranch people, and we just thought of it as another house, another place to live. . . . I'd heard about the springs, but I didn't believe it." It is easy to imagine how she must have felt, a ranch woman of many years, with a conventional sense of medicine and sickness, when people began showing up on her doorstep asking for help. Many of those people who come to hot springs come as a last resort after all conventional means of treatment have been used with little or no effect. Some come for themselves; others are too sick to come by themselves and are brought by their families. And a few, as in the case of the alcoholic whose story she recounted, are more or less dumped on the doorstep and abandoned. Simply because she was there, many of these people expected her to know something of the springs and how to treat them with the water. Despairing of the situation at first, she said she confided her panic to a friend. "Well," the friend said as comfort, "just do whatever you can do. That's all the doctors ever do anyway."

At first, she did little more than point out where the springs were located and tell those who came to help themselves to the water. But then tragedy struck her family. Walter Babb, apparently a somewhat asocial man who enjoyed most being by himself on the range or in the desert, had spent increasingly long periods of time trapping in Mexico. But it was a shock to Mrs. Babb and a blow to the family structure when he was found dead from a heart attack in Mexico. Then, shortly after receiving the telegram giving her the news of his death, her three sons—Dixie, Irvin, and Wayne—were indicted on charges of cattle smuggling. After the trial, when two were sent to jail and one was in self-exile in Mexico on advice from his lawyer, Mrs. Babb found herself alone and without money for the first time in her life. "I was thirty miles from a town and no money to buy but a few groceries once in a while. And the friends I thought we had run like greased lightning (as they say). The friends I had left could be counted on one hand."

This series of circumstances affected Mrs. Babb's development as a healer in two significant ways. First, it stimulated her to look for ways in which she could make a living on her own. Their livestock had been almost completely wiped out, and many of the Babbs' financial resources had been used up in legal fees. The hotel and springs, she knew, had once been utilized as a source of revenue. After considering the possibilities, she felt that her best course of action would be to put the hotel on a paying basis again. She had had some experience with the motel business in Sierra Blanca and so knew something of basic hostelry. Therefore, she decided to learn as much about the springs and their healing properties as she could so that she could handle the patients who would come and stay. For the next eight years, she set about educating herself, learning as much as she could from the Mexican villagers who lived across the river, from the various patients who came to the springs, from the previous owner of the springs, Mr. Foster, who occasionally visited, and from any books on healing techniques which were recommended to her by various visitors. In addition, she had the practical learning experience of working on a daily basis with those who came to the springs for treatment. Being at a location where hot mineral water occurred, a known component of folk healing techniques for centuries, she acted as a magnet for traditional medicine information from a variety of ethnic sources. These included the fractured Anglo tradition, which could be reconstructed with the daily trial and error of the healer-patient relationship to serve as a guide and with the strong reinforcement of the *curanderismo* tradition from right across the river.

The second result of the Babbs' reversal in fortune was a shift in Jewel Babb's position in the Anglo community. She was isolated from the other ranching families, and at the same time, because of her lack of transportation and funds, she was more dependent on the villagers in Ojos Calientes across the river from the hot springs. This shift away from the Anglo community was important because, even in the desert isolation of West Texas, the ranchers' value system does not include a place for the faith or folk healer, and natural healing techniques have little or no prestige. Ironically, then, as Mrs. Babb lost prestige within her own community, she was accorded it by the Mexican community in proportion to her expanding knowledge of natural and psychic healing techniques. By living on the border, she was able to develop her healing talents in a climate which both encouraged and rewarded her for her efforts in addition to whatever financial remuneration she might receive from operating the hotel. Her clientele included the Mexican population who accept the faith healer as an integral part of their value system and those Anglos who, for whatever reasons, continued to have some interest in traditional folk medicine which brought them to the hot springs. Many of these Anglos were those who had been isolated from their own value system by a negative diagnosis from Anglo physicians, their cases being declared either hopeless or out of the range of modern medical care, so that some of them had, in effect, been "left for dead" outside ordinary society at this border retreat.

I have said that Mrs. Babb turned to learning the healing techniques utilizing the mineral waters as a method to earn a living. It would be unfair, however, to say that her sole interest in healing was monetary. From her early days, she recalls having a feeling for the sick and wanting to do all she could to help them. When she realized that she would not be able to keep the springs, she did not really consider giving up her healing call. Instead, she began to cast around for other methods of healing, including the zone therapy techniques she learned from one visitor to the springs, an elaborate system similar to Chinese acupuncture in that it is based on a theory that nerve endings at various points in the feet and other parts of the body connect with internal organs and that manipulation of these points can bring relief to the affected areas otherwise unreachable through massage. And when she left the hot springs, she was very different from the simple ranching woman who had first arrived. In the course of time, Mrs. Babb had learned as much as anyone who had ever been associated with the hot springs about how to use the mud, mosses, and waters. She had learned massage, including zone therapy and other advanced massage techniques. In addition to these natural healing techniques, Mrs. Babb had gradually become aware, according to her testimony, of psychic powers which were growing within her, enabling her to heal people without touching them or otherwise administering to them.

Her subsequent years of living alone at the tie house in the desert were a time of additional study and quiet meditation, increasing her faith in God's power to care for her, a belief she was able to pass on to those she treated. And, in spite of her isolation, her reputation as a healer continued to grow. At present, at her home in Valentine, she receives a small but steady stream of those seeking her help.

Those members of the border community who comprise the largest part of Mrs. Babb's clientele come primarily from two distinct groups. One is the large group of Mexicans who reside on either side of the river. Their reliance upon *curanderismo* is very strong, and although some research in Texas has indicated a tendency among Mexican Americans to "shop around" among available healers,[19] those healers who operate within the traditional value structure and at the same time produce results are doubly honored. It has been hypothesized that this winning combination is what obtained Don Pedrito Jaramillo his posthumous status as folk saint in the southern border area.[20] The second large group is comprised of Anglos who, for various reasons, find themselves outside the prevailing Anglo value system.

Most of these Anglos could be loosely defined as "counterculture" and are scattered along the border area primarily in and around the city of El Paso and its surrounding villages. Although study of this group is practically nonexistent, I think it would be fair to say that, by and large, their value system in regard to traditional medicine is still forming, although they do have certain strongly held beliefs in the value of natural products for healing, ecological concerns which include an interest in hot springs and other natural phenomena, and a tendency to seek unified systems, as exemplified in the term "holistic health."

In addition to this border community, Mrs. Babb's clientele also includes individuals from various parts of the country who either came into contact with her during her stay at the hot springs or have heard about her through friends. This group of clients are generally Anglo and are afflicted with a variety of problems which have not responded, for various reasons, to modern medicine. Their knowledge and belief in traditional medicine no doubt vary from individual to individual. By and large, however, they have turned to this source of medical relief as a "last resort" and are primarily interested in obtaining results which have not been forthcoming from more accepted forms of medicine.

Mrs. Babb's healing techniques have drawn together certain strands of the Anglo folk healing tradition and certain border values in a way which appeals not only to her Anglo clientele but also to the more specific demands of her Mexican clientele for medicine administered within a certain tradition. At the basic level, she provides the services which the folk healer has always provided and which gratify the expectations of all three groups of clientele: a healing method which will treat the whole person. Jerome Frank, in his study of faith healing, found a common base in many folk healing traditions—that of seeing illness in a holistic sense with a concern for calling out the patient's natural healing powers, the healers acting primarily as a conduit, seeing themselves as bringing supernatural forces to bear on the patient. The healing ritual is calculated to reinforce the image of the healer as a powerful ally in the patient's struggle to combat the forces of his or her own illness, and the healer might call upon both the patient and the patient's family to help in this struggle, so that the patient's activities help to counteract a sense of helplessness and hopelessness and to demonstrate an ability to still be of use to one's self as well as to others.[21] These techniques are of primary importance to that group of Mrs. Babb's patients who have been unable to find relief from conventional methods. In Mrs. Babb, they find a healer who assures them that healing is always possible and that she will work with them for as long as is necessary in order to effect a cure. That such assurances from the healer are effective is amply demonstrated by the (literal) barrel of letters Mrs. Babb keeps at her Valentine house from across the country, testifying to various cures and thanking her for her help.

In addition to her basic appeal as folk healer for those interested in "last resort" medicine, Mrs. Babb satisfies the more specific expectations of her Mexican clientele, while at the same time providing a model for folk healing to which the Anglo counterculture can relate.

First, the way in which she gradually became aware of her calling is consistent with the *curandero* tradition. It is not unusual for *curanderos* to realize their divine power late in life, and professional status is rarely attained before middle age. In the San Antonio survey of *curanderos*,[22] the median age was sixty-three years, the age range from forty to ninety-two. Usually the gift of curing is revealed through a dream, a vision, a voice, or the development of a deep understanding of the sick, and many times it is associated with a grave illness of the curers themselves or one of their family. Practical necessity was also found to play a part in some cases, as when the healers find themselves in an environment where no medical facilities are available or when a knowledge of first-aid on the job is found to be necessary. However, the full-time healer almost always ascribes healing power to a divine vision or visitation and afterward usually symbolizes and commemorates this visitation with an image of the divine visitant, the picture or statue of a saint, prominently displayed. A few, such as the folk saint Don Pedrito Jaramillo, ascribed their power directly to God, with no intervening agency, so that no image was necessary.

Mrs. Babb was over fifty years old before she became interested in healing more than her immediate family, and then there was no sensationalism in her call, which was realized gradually. First, she felt she had been "placed" where sick were brought to her unbidden for healing. The pressures upon her to "do something to help" would be much the same as if grave illness had befallen her family. In addition, this pressure was put upon her coincidentally with her own need for developing a livelihood outside her husband's protection and an identity of her own outside the one automatically conferred upon her by the community, which had been lost upon her family's fall from grace. Then, after the accumulation of practical knowledge attached to the use of the springs, the call culminated in the recognition through an outside agency (i.e., the man at the baths) of her psychic power to "touch without touching," much the equivalent of the outside agency of dream or voice. This call was further corroborated by the vision given to her of the little men and their lights. Although spirit helpers of this type are not necessarily within the Catholic tradition, they are a part of the Indian tradition, called *enanitos* and reported in various parts of Mexico.[23] In addition, a spirit helper similar to the one she describes as being "such an ancient age, wrinkled all over" sounds similar to a helper reported by a spiritualist *curandero* whom the informant called "el grande," indicating that he was about forty thousand years old.[24] The use of "spirit helpers," then, transcends specific cultural tradition and, in fact, are familiar within the framework of spiritualistic *curanderismo*. On the other hand, no Catholic image, which might make uncomfortable her Anglo clientele with predominantly Protestant origins, is utilized in Mrs. Babb's home.

Second, the way in which Mrs. Babb handles the monetary aspects of her calling is characteristic of the Mexican *curandero*, relying on mutual good will and an exchange of services more than cash remuneration. Although Mrs. Babb's initial impetus in attempting to learn the techniques of healing was that of financial necessity, she gradually came to a personal realization that making money by healing was against God's will. At present, she never asks money for healing, although she will accept whatever payment is made, whether it is money, goods, or an exchange of work. This is very much in the tradition of *curanderismo*, which insists that healing ability is a gift from God and that money should not be made from it. Usually the *curandero* does not charge a fee; however, the patient leaves an offering or brings small gifts, such as a chicken, vegetables, or a bundle of wood. This method is also highly satisfactory to Mrs. Babb's counterculture clientele who, as a group, have a suspicion of the monied economy and tend to support cooperative and communal enterprises. In addition, this method enables her to work on a long-term basis with chronically incapacitated patients who might otherwise be unable to afford such continued services.

In a typical exchange of services, one woman from El Paso, Terry W., recently lived with Mrs. Babb for a month, primarily to learn about the care and treatment of goats. In exchange for her instruction, Terry planted a spring garden for Mrs. Babb, mended the chimney where it had become unchinked, and performed various minor chores in the house. Another exchange was clearly delineated in a letter Mrs. Babb wrote in May 1977. The patient outlined what he would do for Mrs. Babb, and she in turn outlined what she was doing for him:

> Saturday evening late an old man drove up. Use to work for Diamond Head Corporation. I'd worked with him three years ago. He told me if I'd give him some foot massages, he'd fix pipes to sink, put in more lights, and do work for me to repay me. So he fixed the pipes under the sink. Now it don't leak. I just need the toilet fixed now. And I'm having a time with him, as he's so stiff. He has brain damage, tumor in right shoulder, bad back. Hernia. And muscles of right arm are as stiff as can be. So looks like it's gonna be several more days' hard work even to make any showing. Yesterday I gave him a form of exorcism. Seemed the best of all, as this morning he said his head was not so heavy.

Third, the materials used by Mrs. Babb for healing purposes are familiar ones in the *curanderismo* tradition and are generally approved as being efficacious for the treatment of disease. Although Mrs. Babb has always expressed an interest in the plants of the area, I think it would be fair to say that she has never become adept in herbal remedies, relying more on the old Anglo household standbys, such as coal oil, as in the case of her goatherder's accident at the tie house. But the use of herbs is only one part of the *curanderismo* tradition. There is also a large emphasis on the curative powers of water and massage. *Curanderos* use hot and cold water baths and heat applications in numerous treatments. Hot sand or a heating pad is used for rheumatism; nosebleeds are treated with cold baths; sweat baths and vapor baths are routinely administered; nervousness is treated by regular hot baths to open the pores, followed by cold baths to close them, in order to allow the nerves to breathe. This use of water to effect body temperature change stems from the Hippocratic medical tradition, a tradition which Anglos share, which held that the body should balance hot and cold qualities associated with the four humors and that illness is an imbalance resulting in either a hot or cold condition. Massage is also used extensively to distend and warm the nerves and is good for pain, joint trouble, and lumps under the skin. Manual pressure is used to rearrange the parts of the body that have gotten out of place. Aches and pains are routinely treated by massaging the muscles with snake oil purchased in the herb stores.

In addition, there can be an equal reliance on eggs, earth, modern medicine available over the counter at drugstores, holy water or water blessed by the *curandero*, printed prayers, and holy objects. A traditional curer can be a general practitioner or a specialist, some common specialists being *parteras* (midwives), *hueseros* (bone healers), and specialists in divination. Some specialize in one healing element, the most common one, according to one survey, being water, "probably because of the ancient Mexican tradition that water is a holy and purifying element."[25] This reverence for water's curative powers is widespread, with common references to it in *The Golden Bough* and is an integral part of Anglo tradition, so that the decoration and celebration of certain holy wells and fountains in England are observed still today. Don Pedrito Jaramillo, the Healer of Los Olmos, was a water specialist prescribing a variety of cures all involving water in some way, from baths once a day for sunstroke to the dunking of a paralytic in the Rio Grande. It is quite possible that the proximity of the Rio Grande, or any other special body of water, would be an additional encouragement to a water specialty.

Mrs. Babb, then, can be seen as a hot springs specialist who has developed the additional specialty of "healing with the mind." Her extensive use of hot springs water also piques the interest of many of her counterculture clientele, who are concerned with recovering the knowledge, both Anglo and Indian, of how to effectively use naturally occurring phenomena for healing purposes. There has also been a growing interest among this group in massage techniques, and several people from the El Paso area, including Eleanor T., the woman who first introduced me to Mrs. Babb, have come to her for lessons in manipulation techniques.

No doubt, the most exotic of Mrs. Babb's healing techniques is that of "healing with the mind," a power which she most commonly visualizes as radiating from the palms of her hands when she raises them in the air, pointed in the direction of the patient. In this manner, her "spirit helpers" are released and then massage the affected parts of the patient's body. This technique is probably an extension of the belief in the "laying on of hands," which is given credence in many folk healing traditions and is common to both Anglo and Mexican folk medicine. Tribute in Mexico is paid to those *curanderos* who are exceptionally competent by attributing to them the gift of the *manos santos*, or "blessed hands." In one interview with a *curandero*,[26] emphasis was placed on the necessity of establishing a psychic link between healer and patient, transferring healing energy from one to the other, which is best done by passing the hands over the troubled area. In the Anglo tradition, this basic technique, with minor variations, is utilized in various Protestant healing sects through the "laying on of hands" administered either by the minister alone or with the help of members of the congregation who have demonstrated strong faith, as well as folk healers in various parts of the country. A Canadian folk healer, Uncle Jim, quivers his left hand over the affected area.[27] And pow-wowers pass their hands, sometimes in elaborate gestures, over the affected areas while reciting charms or Bible verses. Not only is healing power transmitted to the patient in this method but, according to many folk traditions, if the healer is not careful the power of the disease can also be transmitted through this link to the healer, so that there is an element of risk involved, as with the story Mrs. Babb gave of the man whom she tried to cure across the river, only to find that the heat of his disease mounted her arms. A remarkably similar story was recorded by James Mooney as the result of an interview in 1889 with an Appalachian healer who cured with herbs but also had the power to cure by the laying on of hands:

> On one occasion he described in detail his method of curing by the touch. The patient is stretched out on the bed, suffering, let us suppose, from rheumatism. The doctor approaches and lays both hands, palms downward, upon the breast of the sick man. He then draws his hands slowly down along the body of the patient, and repeats the operation until he feels the disease enter at the tips of his own fingers, then mount gradually into his arms, and so pass into his body. At first he can shake off the disease current from his fingers, as one shakes drops of water from the hand, but as it becomes stronger it fills his whole body and thrills every nerve, until at last he can endure it no longer, but must rush out of the house to the nearest stream . . . and there washes off the deadly influence by repeated ablutions.[28]

The belief in "long-distance" healing can be seen as a variation of the same technique, but with more physical distance between the healer and patient, and again is a commonly held belief in both Mexican and Anglo folk cultures. Don Pedrito Jaramillo was frequently requested to administer long-distance cures and many of these cures were reported to be successful. One Texas man was supposed to be able to cure screwworm in an animal at a long distance if the animal was described to him, including where the cut was and how bad the worms were.[29] An Oklahoma man, Uncle Perry Fields, is reported to cure thrush in babies long distance when their mothers write him with the infants' names and ages.[30] Many radio evangelistic faith healers operate within this belief structure, sometimes sending the petitioner a blessed object to aid in the long-distance cure, other times simply promising to pray for the cure at a certain time.

These healing techniques then, though seemingly exotic, are well known to Mexicans and Anglos alike. Both the Mexican villagers with their belief in supernatural powers and the Anglos who are interested in psychic phenomena can readily accept this kind of healing as being within a widespread and respected healing tradition.

These elements—the divine call with emphasis on the healer as a medium through which healing powers are channeled, the mutual exchange of services, the uses of manipulation and water as well as other natural elements, and a belief in supernatural powers which can manifest themselves either through the laying on of hands or through a long-distance healing—form the basis of Mrs. Babb's healing techniques and ritual. Their appeal is transcultural, so that, although one group of patients might respond for slightly different reasons than another, the basic techniques lend themselves to a variety of cultural expectations. When one old grandmother in New Mexico was once questioned about how she could believe in both Catholicism and the Old Religion, she replied, "Los dos corren juntos," and made a motion with her two hands as if two animals were running neck and neck.[31] Much the same could be said of the Anglo and Mexican folk medicine traditions—"the two run together." And on the border, where cultures come into daily contact with each other, when tradition is weak on one side it might be encouraged by the stronger tradition on the other. This, of course, is speculation: at the hot springs it is difficult, if not impossible, to decide definitely what medical lore first belonged to whom. But this is sure: Mrs. Babb is a true representative of a border culture which has provided a climate for bringing traditions together, just as she has been able to bring people together of differing ethnic backgrounds in a combined clientele. Mrs. Jewel Babb: border healing woman—a special breed of woman in a very special part of the world.

Notes

2. Early Childhood

1. Flash flooding has historically been a major hazard in this part of the country. One flooding of record is documented in the W. D. Smithers Photographic Collection at the University of Texas Humanities Research Center, #2939. It occurred when the Sixth Cavalry set up a tie camp at the Evett's Ranch outside Valentine in 1916. Unfortunately, the men made the mistake of building their camp in the bed of the Diez y Ocho Creek, which became a raging torrent with the first big rain, washing their tie camp into the Rio Grande about nine miles away.

2. The mountain laurel, according to Sadie Hatfield's "Folklore of Texas Plants," is also called, variously, mescal bean, "big drunk bean," goat bean, and *frijallito*. Only half a bean crushed and ground and put into liquor mash is said to make a man wild as well as drunk. The Texas law against marijuana includes the mountain laurel. See "Folklore of Texas Plants," in *Texas Folk and Folklore*, ed. Mody C. Boatright, p. 277.

3. This is a reference to the pressure points in the feet, one of the underlying principles of zone therapy, Mrs. Babb's system of massage.

4. *Oleracea*, or purslane.

5. *Amaranthus retroflexus*, also called pigweed, amaranth, and red-root.

6. Horehound, or *Marrubium vulgare*, has traditionally been used for the treatment of throat and lung ailments, including colds and croup. In large amounts, it is used as a laxative.

7. Tallow.

3. Healing with the Mind

1. This material is directly transcribed from recorded conversation.

2. Although pokeweed, *Rivina humilis*, is widely known in folk medicine as a blood purifier, precautions should be taken in its use, as the leaves are purportedly poisonous unless picked young and cooked properly. The root is also used as a cure for fistula when boiled, mashed, and applied hot, while the cooking water is used to bathe the affected area.

3. This material is directly transcribed from recorded conversation.

4. *Sassafras variifolium*; the dried bark of the root is a common diaphoretic in folk medicine, boiled and steeped for tea.

5. The full name is cascara sagrada, meaning literally "sacred bark." A buckthorn (*Rhamnus purshiana*), its bark was commonly dried in the western states and used as a laxative. An extract made from the bark is still used in patent medicines, including Dr. Pierce's Golden Medical Discovery, purportedly good for poor appetite or poor digestion.

6. Mercurous chloride, much used in medicine as a mercurial, purgative, and anthelmintic.

7. Black Draught is still on the market, including Black Draught tablets and Syrup of Black Draught for children. Its label lists one active ingredient: senna, probably certain species of cassia (esp. *Cassia acutifolia* and *C. angustifolia*), commonly used as a purgative.

8. A preparation made from extracting a proteolytic enzyme which is secreted in the stomachs of pigs, sheep, or calves and used as a digestive.

9. This material is directly transcribed from recorded conversation.

4. A Ranch Marriage

1. Judge Roy Bean was commissioned as a justice of the peace by the ranger force in 1882, and until his death in 1903 he was known as "the law west of the Pecos." His Langtry headquarters are preserved as a historical site, including a small frame shack with a covered porch sporting several signs reading: THE JERSEY LILLY. JUDGE ROY BEAN NOTARY PUBLIC. LAW WEST OF THE PECOS.

2. *Gayuba, Arbutus texana*, also called Madrona, Naked Indian, or redberried arbutus.

3. Birth marking beliefs are widespread and found in diverse cultures. For a good discussion of Anglo beliefs, see William W. Bass, "Birthmarks among the Folk," *Tennessee Folklore Society Bulletin* 25 (March 1959): 1–6.

4. A commercial preparation using mustard seed as an active ingredient, which produces heat when applied to the affected area.

5. Sore mouth is a common goat disease in the border area. Mexican goatherds believe it is caused by grazing while the dew is still on the grass. One remedy given for it in Frost Woodhull's ranch *remedios* is to mix coal oil and lard half and half, with one pound of salt added to every gallon, then to wash mouth, nose, and tongue with the mixture. See Frost Woodhull, "Ranch *Remedios*," in *Man, Bird and Beast*, ed. J. Frank Dobie, p. 46.

6. The bark from the black jack or cherry tree is also used for diarrhea, as are mesquite gum and horehound leaves.

5. The Trappers

1. The quoted material in this chapter has been transcribed from recorded conversation.

2. *Echinocereus enneacanthus*, called also strawberry cactus, grows a delicious fruit with a strawberry flavor.

3. Prickly pear, or *Opuntia humifusa*, is also pounded up and mashed to use as a poultice for snakebite. The ripe fruit, or tuna, is made into tea to cure gallstones.

4. *Sanguinaria canadensis*, also called bloodwort and knotgrass, is known in the Rio Grande region as a burn remedy—a tea made from the root to bathe the burn, or the actual root used as a poultice. Taken in small amounts, it stimulates the gastric juices but more can be poisonous. It also causes sneezing, which loosens accumulated phlegm.

5. Soapweed is usually the name given in the northern border region to Spanish bayonet, dagger plant, or *Yucca glauca* and is used to wash the hair and body. The *Yucca brevifolia* is more commonly called Joshua tree and is not known generally as soapweed. There are many species of yucca varying in size from one to eight feet with numerous useful properties.

6. *Dasylirion texanum*, also known as saw yucca or sotol, is used as fence posts and thatch for roofs because of its tough, slender stalk. The beverage made from its head is known as sotol or sotol mescal.

7. From the 1920s to the 1940s, the extraction of wax from the candelilla plant was big business on the border. Now, however, there is a cheaper synthetic substitute and only a few dozen wax camps are left along the river. For a complete discussion of the extraction process, see Joe S. Graham, "Tradition and the Candelilla Wax Industry," in *Some Still Do: Essays on Texas Customs*, ed. Francis Edward Abernethy, pp. 39–54.

6. Changing Circumstances

1. Mrs. Babb indicated a spot several inches above the stomach area.

2. I have been unable to verify the name of the village, but it has been referred to in the literature as Ojo Caliente, Ojos Calientes, and Oasis Caliente, all of which may be correct folk variants.

3. The names of all the villagers have been changed to protect them from possible incrimination.

4. It has been impossible for me to find any record of such a transaction. A local historian, Dogie Wright, says that there was a time in the thirties when there was smallpox across the river in Ojos Calientes. He could remember it because of the stir it made at the springs, as the hotel's clothing and bedding were washed there, although no one from the springs contracted it. But the blanket transaction was unknown to him.

5. These lights are described similarly to the Marfa lights, which have been reported periodically about 150 miles south of the springs; and approximately thirty miles from the springs is Red Light Canyon, named by residents of the area because of the frequency of lights spotted along its sides. The English Department of Sul Ross State University in Alpine, Texas, has an extensive file of such stories.

6. The association of light with the soul is found frequently in folktales, although it is difficult in Mrs. Babb's various accounts of these lights to differentiate between what is supposed to be a ghost and what would be considered "familiar spirits." This is apparently a common characteristic of such stories, noted in Stith Thompson, *Motif-Index to Folk-Literature*, p. 361.

7. The Hot Springs

1. There are springs found in natural complexes in other parts of the country which are also described by their users as having diverse healing properties. The seven springs in the Heber Springs complex in Arkansas are an example. According to one informant: "The eye spring cured sore eyes, the stomach spring cured ulcers, the black sulphur, red sulphur and white sulphur springs got their names because you put a coin in there, a silver coin, and it turns it those colors, the iron spring cured anemia, the magnesium spring cured whatever was left" (Nancy McDonough, *Garden Sass: A Catalog of Arkansas Folkways*, p. 252).

2. The exception made of cancer is common also in *curanderismo*. Many *curanderos* describe cancer as a punishment from God and therefore impossible to cure by natural means. They cite the fact that Anglo doctors can rarely cure cancer as proof of its supernatural cause.

3. There is a certificate of analysis for the spring water in Jewel Babb's possession given to her by H. L. Hunt, who had the water analyzed when he bought the property. The analysis shows that all the water is high in mineral content, with magnesium bicarbonate, sodium bicarbonate, sodium sulfate, and sodium chloride the most significant and common to all three of the springs analyzed.

4. Hot springs have been known for their purgative qualities for centuries. In 1567, a Dr. Turner recommended the waters of Bath for:

> The vayne appetite of going to the stoole when
> a man can do nothing when he commeth there.

And one of the main reasons for Epsom's fame as a spa was its purgative qualities, so renowned that its name was attached to the famous purgative Epsom Salts (John Camp, *Magic, Myth and Medicine*, p. 150).

The necessity to periodically purge the body is consistent with *curandero* belief, which holds that free passage is necessary in the body and that obstruction will lead to deposits, or residuals, which cause disease.

5. Wayland Hand has compiled a list of common folk inhalants in respiratory disorders, ranging from curing whooping cough by inhaling the ammoniacal fumes of a gas works to curing asthma by burning a buzzard's wing feathers under the nose. Although the fumes of hot springs are not listed in his range of inhalants, several of the listings call for a combination of heat and moisture. See Wayland D. Hand and Marjorie Griffin, "Inhalants in Respiratory Disorders," *Journal of American Folklore* 77 (July–September 1964): 259–261.

The mixture of inhalation and sweating therapy is a common treatment that *curanderos* and other folk healers use for viral upper respiratory infections. Stones are heated with various herbs in boiling water, and the patient leans over the vapors.

6. *Curanderos* often use a hot water bath with rosemary as a treatment for infertility, as the heat, reportedly, warms the "cold womb" (Ari Kiev, *Curanderismo: Mexican-American Folk Psychiatry*, p. 132).

7. The curative powers of soda have been relied upon by pioneer families for years, used for such divergent problems as indigestion, rheumatism, bad breath, external wounds, and skin diseases. In New Mexico, the crude sodium bicarbonate which forms on the banks of mineral springs is called *tequesquite* and is scraped up by the Indians and used both for cooking and as a medicine for indigestion.

8. "Radiation Intensity Survey of Indian Hot Springs," compiled by geophysicist Philip K. Sampler, shows the radiation count at the springs to be thirteen times higher in some places than in the surrounding river area. He notes that nowhere else in the area is there any substantial increase in radiation other than at the springs, which might indicate ancient springs buried beneath the present alluvium.

9. Herbalist Jethro Kloss also recommended hot baths in the alleviation of diabetes, alternated with cold showers and supplemented with hot teas made from red raspberry leaves, blueberry leaves, dandelion root, or pleurisy root (*Back to Eden*, p. 402). This treatment is essentially the same as what many *curanderos* prescribe.

10. Hot springs in general have been noted for their benefit to healthy skin. W. D. Smithers, who in his lifetime recorded many remedies that he had observed along the Rio Grande border, tells of one Mexican family he knew that lived close to a hot springs: "That water must have had good benefits, for the complexion and color of his children was much lighter and clearer than the average" (*Nature's Pharmacy and the Border Trading Posts*, p. 52).

11. Dudley R. Dobie, in his Foreword to Smithers' book, notes Smithers' belief expressed during a conversation between the two men in the curative powers of water and its vegetation: "Most Texas ranchmen will tell you about finding a wounded deer lying in a shady, cool pool of water, with its wound under water. This instinct for cure might have one of three meanings, or all three: first the wound is protected from flies; second, the coolness of the water naturally subdues fever. And finally, Smithers wonders whether there is a penicillin type cure fermented from the decayed vegetation in the pool of water. Mr. Smithers states that he has heard that the early American Indians and the more nomadic Mexicans, who were often one and the same people, resorted to this type of treatment for serious wounds that required weeks of healing" (ibid., p. 12).

12. Holly is Mrs. Babb's granddaughter, who stayed with her various times at the springs.

8. Alone on the Rio Grande

1. Capt. W. J. Maltby, *Captain Jeff, or Frontier Life in Texas with the Texas Rangers*, p. 143.

2. A detailed account of this kind of recreation is given by Zola Davis, whose family spent vacations around the turn of the century at the hot springs in the Big Bend area, known at the time as Langford Hot Springs, in "Zola (Harmon) Davis Recalls Early Days," *Alpine Avalanche*, June 28, 1962, p. 6-F.

3. Additional statistical data on Indian Hot Springs can be found in William Kaysing's survey of hot springs, *Thermal Springs of the Western United States*, p. 103.

9. Desert Years

1. I have included a more thorough discussion of this structure in an article entitled "Texas Tie Houses," in *Built in Texas*, ed. Francis Abernethy, pp. 85–91. An excellent general source on railroad tie structures is Roger L. Welsch, "Railroad-Tie Construction on the Pioneer Plains," *Western Folklore* 35 (April 1976): 151–152.

2. A southern Anglo term which means to burn a piece of wood in the middle rather than chopping it in half with an axe.

3. This has long been a popular area for peyote hunters. The Comanche chief Quanah Parker came into the area in 1884 looking for the "gift-of-god" cactus which is said to grow from the Davis Mountains down the Rio Grande to the Gulf Coast (*The Big Bend Country of Texas and Big Bend National Park*, p. 37).

4. "Evening" in West Texas dialect is commonly used to mean "afternoon."

5. The reference is to the biblical David who, as the story goes, was the youngest son of Jesse and therefore in charge of herding the sheep. Although he apparently had received little formal education, he was chosen by God through the prophet Samuel over his older, more educated brothers to first serve King Saul and later to become king himself because, according to the biblical text, "he behaved himself wisely" (I Samuel 18:5).

6. It is Mrs. Babb's belief that we live in apocalyptic times. She has no specific prophetic vision but will frequently refer in conversation to this "time of chaos" in the near future as a matter of fact.

7. Another Texas faith healer, a Mrs. DuBose in Gary, has also mentioned the Ezekiel Bible verse in passing, but she, too, does not use it herself (Fred Hardin, Norbert Korzeniewski, Tommy Hopper, and David Hammers, "Faith Healing," in *Some Still Do*, ed. Abernethy, pp. 124–131).

In other parts of the country, including Pennsylvania, Michigan, and the Appalachian mountain region, bloodstopping with the use of either a Bible verse, such as this one, or a charm is still well known. In his study of bloodstoppers, Richard Dorson met several people who either had purportedly witnessed bloodstopping or could stop blood themselves (*Bloodstoppers and Bearwalkers*).

10. Afterword

1. Ronald H. Davidson and Richard Day, *Symbol and Realization: A Contribution to the Study of Magic and Healing*, p. 2.
2. James Owen Sherman, "Spiritualistic Curanderismo," pp. 2–3.
3. Don Yoder, "Folk Medicine," in *Folklore and Folklife*, ed. Richard M. Dorson, pp. 191–212.
4. Clarence Meyer, *American Folk Medicine*, p. 3.
5. William A. Owens, "Seer of Corsicana," in *And Horns on Toads*, ed. Mody Boatright, Wilson M. Hudson, and Allen Maxwell, pp. 14–31.
6. For a brief but inclusive history of the war waged against traditional medicine in the South, see Peter Wood, "People's Medicine in the Early South," *Southern Exposure* 6 (Summer 1978): 50–53.
7. B. Eliot Wigginton, "Two Faith Healers Tell Exactly How It's Done," *North Carolina Folklore* 16 (November 1968): 163–165.
8. Woodhull, "Ranch *Remedios*," p. 67.
9. Ibid.
10. Ibid., p. 70.
11. Ibid., p. 57.
12. Ibid., p. 23.
13. Ibid., p. 10.
14. *Susto* is a condition believed to be caused by fright or sudden trauma which causes the soul to leave the body; the healer must put it back. *Empacho* is believed to be caused by indigested food forming a ball in the digestive tract which must be dissolved and removed. *Mal de ojo*, or "evil eye," is a declining condition caused in a patient when one either wittingly or unwittingly has given him or her the evil eye. It is generally held that looking at a person or a person's possessions with envy and afterward failing to touch the person to remove the effect will cause *mal de ojo*.
15. Arthur J. Rubel, "Concepts of Disease in a Mexican-American Community in Texas," *American Anthropologist* 62 (October 1962): 795–814.
16. Daniel Alegria, Ernesto Guerra, Cervando Martinez, Jr., and George G. Meyer, "El Hospital Invisible: A Study of Curanderismo," *Archives of General Psychiatry* 34 (November 1977): 1356.
17. Paul D. Gray, *Distribution of Physicians in Texas*, pp. 18, 52.
18. Fred Pass, ed., *Texas Almanac and State Industrial Guide, 1978–79*, p. 309.
19. Arthur J. Rubel, *Across the Tracks: Mexican-Americans in a Texas City*, p. 177.
20. See Octavio Ignacio Romano's study of Don Pedrito in "Charismatic

Medicine, Folk-Healing and Folk Sainthood," *American Anthropologist* 67 (October 1965): 1151–1173.

21. Jerome D. Frank, *Persuasion and Healing*, p. 47.

22. Alegria, Guerra, Martinez, and Meyer, "El Hospital Invisible," p. 1356.

23. Sherman, "Spiritualistic Curanderismo," pp. 13–14.

24. Ibid., p. 57.

25. William Madsen, "Value Conflicts and Folk Psychotherapy in South Texas," in *Magic, Faith and Healing: Studies in Primitive Psychiatry Today*, ed. Ari Kiev, p. 430.

26. Kiev, *Curanderismo*, pp. 137–138.

27. Michael Owen Jones, *Why Faith Healing?* p. 13.

28. James Moony, "Folk-Lore of the Carolina Mountains," *Journal of American Folklore* 2 (April–June 1889): 102.

29. Woodhull, "Ranch *Remedios*," p. 14.

30. Walter R. Smith, "Northwestern Oklahoma Folk Cures," in *Man, Bird and Beast*, ed. Dobie, p. 79.

31. Carobeth Laird, *Encounter with an Angry God*, p. 94.

Bibliography

Abernethy, Francis Edward, ed. *Built in Texas*. Waco: E-Heart Press, 1979.
———, ed. *Some Still Do: Essays on Texas Customs*. Austin: Encino Press, 1975.
Alegria, Daniel, Ernesto Guerra, Cervando Martinez, Jr., and George G. Meyer. "El Hospital Invisible: A Study of Curanderismo." *Archives of General Psychiatry* 34 (November 1977): 1354–1359.
Bass, William W. "Birthmarks among the Folk." *Tennessee Folklore Society Bulletin* 25 (March 1959): 1–6.
Baun, Paul F., and Newman Ivey White, eds. *The Frank C. Brown Collection of North Carolina Folklore*. Durham, N.C., 1952–1961.
The Big Bend Country of Texas and Big Bend National Park. N.p.: Continental Publishers by the Park Service, n.d.
Black, William George. *Folk-Medicine: A Chapter in the History of Culture*. New York: Taplinger Publishing Co., 1973.
Boatright, Mody C., ed. *The Healer of Los Olmos and Other Mexican Lore*. Dallas: Southern Methodist University Press, 1951.
———, ed. *Texas Folk and Folklore*. Dallas: Southern Methodist University Press, 1954.
———, Wilson M. Hudson, and Allen Maxwell, eds. *And Horns on Toads*. Dallas: Southern Methodist University Press, 1959.
Bourke, John H. "Popular Medicine, Customs and Superstitions of the Rio Grande." *Journal of American Folklore* 7 (April–June 1894): 119–146.
Browne, Ray B. *Popular Beliefs from Alabama*. Berkeley, 1958.
Camp, John. *Magic, Myth and Medicine*. New York: Taplinger Publishing Co., 1973.
Clark, Margaret. *Health in the Mexican-American Culture*. Berkeley and Los Angeles: University of California Press, 1959.
Curtin, L. S. M. *Healing Herbs of the Upper Rio Grande*. Santa Fe: Laboratory of Anthropology, 1947.
Davidson, Ronald H., and Richard Day. *Symbol and Realization: A Contribution to the Study of Magic and Healing*. Berkeley: Center for South and Southeast Asian Studies, 1974.

Dobie, J. Frank, ed. *Man, Bird and Beast*. Austin: Texas Folklore Society, 1930.
Dorson, Richard M. *Bloodstoppers and Bearwalkers*. Cambridge, Mass.: Harvard University Press, 1956.
Ehrenreich, Barbara, and Deirdre English. *Complaints and Disorders: The Sexual Politics of Sickness*. New York: Feminist Press, 1973.
———, and ———. *Witches, Midwives and Nurses: A History of Women Healers*. New York: Feminist Press, 1974.
Elliott, Mrs. Dee. Personal interview by Pat Ellis Taylor. Sierra Blanca, Texas, March 5, 1977.
Fielder, Mildred. *Plant Medicine and Folklore*. New York: Winchester Press, 1975.
Flipper, Henry O. *Negro Frontiersman: Western Memoirs of Henry O. Flipper, 1877–1916*. El Paso: Texas Western Press, 1963.
Foster, George M. "Relationships between Spanish and Spanish-American Folk Medicine." *Journal of American Folklore* 66 (July–September 1953): 201–247.
Frank, Jerome D. *Persuasion and Healing*. Baltimore: Johns Hopkins University Press, 1961.
Frazer, Sir James George. *The New Golden Bough*. New York: Criterion Books, 1959.
Gravell, Madge Smith. Personal interview by Sam Tidwell. Alpine, Texas, Sul Ross University, March 1970.
Gray, Paul D. *Distribution of Physicians in Texas*. Austin: Texas Medical Association, 1973.
Grieve, M. *A Modern Herbal*. New York: Hafner Publishing Co., 1967.
Gusfield, Joseph R. "Tradition and Modernity: Misplaced Polarities in the Study of Social Change." *American Journal of Sociology* 72 (January 1967): 351–362.
Hand, Wayland, ed. *The Frank C. Brown Collection of North Carolina Folklore*. Vol. VI. Durham, N.C.: Duke University Press, 1964.
———, and Marjorie Griffin. "Inhalants in Respiratory Disorders." *Journal of American Folklore* 77 (July–September 1964): 259–261.
Hultin, Neil. "Some Aspects of Eighteenth-Century Folk Medicine." *Southern Folklore Quarterly* 38 (Summer 1974): 199–209.
Ingham, John M. "On Mexican Folk Medicine." *American Anthropologist* 52 (February 1970): 76–87.
Jones, Michael Owen. "Toward an Understanding of Folk Medical Beliefs." *North Carolina Folklore* 15 (May 1967): 23–27.
———. *Why Faith Healing?* Ottawa: National Museums of Canada, 1972.
Kaysing, William C. *Thermal Springs of the Western United States*. Santa Barbara, Calif.: Paradise Publishers, 1970.
Kiev, Ari. *Curanderismo: Mexican-American Folk Psychiatry*. New York: Free Press, 1968.

———, ed. *Magic, Faith and Healing: Studies in Primitive Psychiatry Today*. New York: Free Press, 1964.

Kloss, Jethro. *Back to Eden*. New York: Beneficial Books, 1971.

Laird, Carobeth. *Encounter with an Angry God*. Banning, Calif.: Malki Museum Press, 1975.

Lessa, William A., and Evon Z. Vogt, eds. *Reader in Comparative Religion: An Anthropological Approach*. New York: Harper & Row, 1963.

Lévi-Straus, Claude. *Structural Anthropology*. New York: Basic Books, 1963.

Loeb, E. M. "Shaman and Seer." *American Anthropologist* 31 (January–March 1929): 60–84.

Long, Grady M. "Folk Medicine in McMinn, Polk, Bradley, and Meig Counties, Tennessee, 1910–1927." *Tennessee Folklore Society Bulletin* 28 (March 1962): 8–12.

McDonough, Nancy. *Garden Sass: A Catalog of Arkansas Folkways*. New York: Coward, McCann & Geoghegan, 1975.

Madsen, William. *Mexican-Americans of South Texas*. New York: Holt, Rinehart and Winston, 1964.

Maltby, Capt. W. J. *Captain Jeff, or Frontier Life in Texas with the Texas Rangers*. Colorado, Tex.: Whipley Printing Co., 1906.

Meyer, Clarence. *American Folk Medicine*. New York: Thomas Y. Crowell Co., 1973.

Mooney, James. "Folk-Lore of the Carolina Mountains." *Journal of American Folklore* 2 (April–June 1889): 95–104.

Parr, Jerry S. "Folk Cures in Middle Tennessee." *Tennessee Folklore Society Bulletin* 28 (March 1962): 8–12.

Pass, Fred, ed. *Texas Almanac and State Industrial Guide, 1978–79*. Dallas: A. H. Belo Corp., 1977.

Patterson, Daniel W., ed. *Folklore Studies in Honor of Arthur Palmer Hudson*. Chapel Hill: North Carolina Folklore Society, 1965.

Porter, J. Hampden. "Notes on the Folklore of the Mountain Whites of the Alleghanies." *Journal of American Folklore* 7 (January–March 1894): 105–117.

Ragsdale, Crystal Sasse. *The Golden Free Land*. Austin, Tex.: Landmark Press, 1976.

Randolph, Vance. *Ozark Superstitions*. New York: Dover, 1947.

Ratliff, Rodney. *Return to the Promised Land, Appalachia*. Frankfort: Kentucky Images, 1977.

Risse, Guenter B., Ronald L. Numbers, and Judith Waltzer Leavitt, eds. *Medicine without Doctors*. New York: Science History Publications, 1977.

Rogers, James C. "Talking Out Fire." *North Carolina Folklore* 16 (May 1968): 46–52.

Romano, Octavio Ignacio. "Charismatic Medicine, Folk-Healing and Folk Sainthood." *American Anthropologist* 67 (October 1965): 1151–1173.

———. "Don Pedrito Jaramillo: The Emergence of a Mexican-American

Folk-Saint." Ph.D. Diss., University of California, 1964.
Rubel, Arthur J. *Across the Tracks: Mexican-Americans in a Texas City*. Austin: University of Texas Press, 1966.
———. "Concepts of Disease in a Mexican-American Community in Texas." *American Anthropologist* 62 (October 1962): 795–814.
Sampler, Philip K. "Radiation Intensity Survey of Indian Hot Springs, Hudspeth Co., Texas," March 1968, compiled for H. L. Hunt. Copy on file in the private library of Pat Ellis Taylor.
Saunders, Lyle. "Healing Ways in the Spanish Southwest." In *Patients, Physicians and Illness*, ed. E. Gartly Jaco. New York: Free Press, 1958.
Schultz, Ellen D. *Texas Wild Flowers*. Chicago: Laidlow Brothers, 1928.
Sharon, Douglas G. "Eduardo the Healer." *Natural History* 81 (November 1972): 32–47.
Sherman, James Owen. "Spiritualistic Curanderismo." Ph.D. Diss., United States International University, 1975.
Shipman, Mrs. O. L. *Taming the Big Bend*. N.p., 1926.
Smithers, W. D. *Nature's Pharmacy and the Border Trading Posts*. Sul Ross State College Bulletin, 41, no. 3. Alpine, Tex., September 1, 1961.
Stuart, Jesse. "New Wine in Old Bottles, Part II." *Kentucky Folklore Record* 13 (January–March 1967): 20–24.
Thompson, Stith. *Motif-Index to Folk-Literature*. Bloomington: Indiana University Press, 1955–1958.
Tidwell, Samuel M. "Casi una virgen." Sul Ross University, April 20, 1970.
Tolbert, Frank X. "Hunt Stirs Up Waters of Indian Hot Springs." *Dallas Morning News*, November 19, 1966.
Welsch, Roger L. "Railroad-Tie Construction on the Pioneer Plains." *Western Folklore* 35 (April 1976): 151–152.
Wigginton, B. Eliot, ed. "Faith Healing." In *The Foxfire Book*, pp. 346–368. New York: Anchor Press, 1972.
———. "Two Faith Healers Tell Exactly How It's Done." *North Carolina Folklore* 16 (November 1968): 163–165.
Wilson, Gordan. "Talismans and Magic in Folk Remedies in the Mammoth Cave Region." *Southern Folklore Quarterly* 30 (June 1966): 192–201.
Wood, Peter. "People's Medicine in the Early South." *Southern Exposure* 6 (Summer 1978): 50–53.
Wright, Dogie. Personal interview by Pat Ellis Taylor. Sierra Blanca, Texas, February 18, 1977.
Wright, Mrs. Dogie. Personal interview by Pat Ellis Taylor. Sierra Blanca, Texas, February 18, 1977.
Yoder, Don. "Folk Medicine." In *Folklore and Folklife*, ed. Richard M. Dorson, pp. 191–212. Chicago: University of Chicago Press, 1972.
"Zola 'Harmon' Davis Recalls Early Days." *Alpine Avalanche*, June 28, 1962.